D1055405

FINDING
GOD'S PEACE
in PERILOUS TIMES

FINDING GOD'S PEACE
in PERILOUS TIMES

TYNDALE HOUSE PUBLISHERS, INC.
WHEATON, ILLINOIS

All proceeds from the sale of this book will be donated to a special fund set up by The Salvation Army to assist the families of the victims of the terrorist attacks of September 11, 2001. Neither Tyndale House Publishers nor any of the authors or artists who have contributed to this compilation will receive any profits from the sale of this book.

Visit Tyndale's exciting Web site at www.tyndale.com

Tyndale House thanks each of the authors, artists, publishers, and agents who contributed to this book either by creating new material or by generously granting permission for previously published works to be reprinted. For detailed information about the sources of the devotional material printed in this book, see page 177.

Compiled by Tammy Faxel.

Designed by Julie Chen.

Edited by Daniel Elliott, Jeremy P. Taylor, and Anisa Baker.

Special thanks to L. B. Norton.

Library of Congress Cataloging-in-Publication Data

Finding God's peace in perilous times / [compiled by Tammy Faxel].
    p. cm.
Includes bibliographical references.
ISBN 0-8423-7060-9
1. September 11 Terrorist Attacks, 2001—Prayer-books and devotions—English.   I. Faxel, Tammy.
BV4897.T47 F56 2001

242'.4—dc21   2001006452

Printed in the United States of America

06   05   04   03   02   01
7   6   5   4   3   2   1

This book is humbly dedicated to the memory of all

those lost in the terrorist attacks on the World Trade

Center in New York City, the Pentagon in

Arlington, Virginia, and on United Flight 93,

which crashed in Somerset County, Pennsylvania,

on September 11, 2001. We grieve with the families

whose lives have been forever altered, and we pray

that God in his infinite mercy will grant them his

ultimate peace.

This picture was painted by Ron DiCianni in honor of the many firefighters and other rescue workers who died during the attacks of September 11, 2001. It is presented here in memory of those brave heroes who gave their lives while saving the lives of others.

"Greater love has no one than this, that he lay down his life for his friends."
John 15:13, NIV

CONTENTS

From the Publisher

We are living in a crucial time in our nation's history. The terrorist attacks that destroyed the World Trade Center, damaged the Pentagon, and caused a plane crash in Pennsylvania on September 11, 2001, have changed the way Americans feel about their lives. The lives lost serve as a constant reminder to all of us that life is fragile and can be taken away at any time. The tens of thousands of grieving families, friends, and loved ones of the victims reveal the great need for compassion and support in the wake of such devastation. The outpouring of support and encouragement from across the nation and around the world inspires us to unite as a nation and stand firm against evil. And the many prayers offered on behalf of the victims and their families exhort us to return to our spiritual roots and find the enduring peace that only a loving God can provide. This book is intended to offer hope, encouragement, and spiritual guidance to those facing conflicting thoughts and feelings about this national disaster.

No one has been more tragically affected by the attacks of September 11 than the families of the victims. The devastation of losing a father, mother, child, or sibling is beyond rational comprehension. The burden that many now face of having to provide for a family that has suddenly lost its primary income is unimaginable. That is why neither Tyndale House Publishers nor any of the authors or artists who have contributed to this book are accepting any royalties or profits from its sale. Instead, the proceeds will be donated to The Salvation Army, who will pass it through a special fund directly to the families affected by the attacks.

Tyndale House would like to thank each of the authors, artists, agents, and publishers who have so generously shared their creativity, inspiration, and cooperation as a gift to the victims' families. We would also like to thank those who have been involved in putting together this important book so quickly. Finally, we would like to remind our readers that God is in control and that he loves all of us deeply. Let us not forget the important lessons we have learned through this horrific national ordeal, and let us not fail to acknowledge our dependence upon God's sustaining guidance in our lives. As we strive as a nation to live up to the ideals set in place by our founders, and as we seek as individuals to find answers to the many questions each of us has following this time of grief and pain, let us remember that it is only through God's Son, Jesus Christ, that we can find true peace in these perilous times.

DR. KENNETH N. TAYLOR
CHAIRMAN OF THE BOARD
TYNDALE HOUSE PUBLISHERS

Do It Again, Lord

by Max Lucado

$\mathcal{D}$ear Lord,

We're still hoping we'll wake up. We're still hoping we'll open a sleepy eye and think, *What a horrible dream.*

But we won't, will we, Father? What we saw was not a dream. Planes did gouge towers. Flames did consume our fortress. People did perish. It was no dream, and, dear Father, we are sad.

There is a ballet dancer who will no longer dance and a doctor who will no longer heal. A church has lost her priest; a classroom is minus a teacher. Cora ran a food pantry. Paige was a counselor, and Dana, dearest Father, Dana was only three years old. (Who held her in those final moments?)

We are sad, Father. For as the innocent are buried,

our innocence is buried as well. We thought we were safe. Perhaps we should have known better. But we didn't.

And so we come to you. We don't ask you for help; we beg you for it. We don't request it; we implore it. We know what you can do. We've read the accounts. We've pondered the stories, and now we plead, *Do it again, Lord. Do it again.*

Remember Joseph? You rescued him from the pit. You can do the same for us. Do it again, Lord.

Remember the Hebrews in Egypt? You protected their children from the angel of death. We have children too, Lord. Do it again.

And Sarah. Remember her prayers? You heard them. Joshua? Remember his fears? You inspired him. The women at the tomb? You resurrected their hope. The doubts of Thomas? You took them away. Do it again, Lord. Do it again.

You changed Daniel from a captive into a king's counselor. You took Peter the fisherman and made him Peter the apostle. Because of you David went from herding sheep to leading armies. Do it again, Lord, for we need counselors today. We need apostles. We need leaders. Do it again, dear Lord.

Most of all, do again what you did at Calvary. What we saw here on that Tuesday, you saw there on that Friday. Innocence slaughtered. Goodness murdered. Mothers weeping. Evil dancing. Just as the ash fell on our children, the darkness fell on your Son. Just as our towers were shattered, the very Tower of Eternity was pierced.

And by dusk, heaven's sweetest song was silent, buried behind a rock.

But you did not waver, O Lord. You did not waver. After three days in a dark hole, you rolled the rock and rumbled the earth and turned the darkest Friday into the brightest Sunday. Do it again, Lord. Grant us a September Easter.

We thank you, dear Father, for these hours of unity. Disaster has done what discussion could not. Doctrinal fences have fallen. Republicans are standing with Democrats. Skin colors have been covered by the ash of burning buildings. We thank you for these hours of unity.

And we thank you for these hours of prayer. The enemy sought to bring us to our knees and succeeded. He had no idea, however, that we would kneel before you. And he has no idea what you can do.

Let your mercy be upon our president, vice president,

and their families. Grant to those who lead us wisdom beyond their years and experience. Have mercy upon the souls who have departed and the wounded who remain. Give us grace that we might forgive and faith that we might believe.

And look kindly upon your church. For two thousand years you've used her to heal a hurting world.

Do it again, Lord. Do it again.

Through Christ, amen.

WINNING
THROUGH LOSING

by Bill Hybels

"MY GRACE IS SUFFICIENT FOR YOU, FOR MY POWER IS MADE PERFECT IN WEAKNESS." THEREFORE I WILL BOAST ALL THE MORE GLADLY ABOUT MY WEAKNESSES, SO THAT CHRIST'S POWER MAY REST ON ME. THAT IS WHY, FOR CHRIST'S SAKE, I DELIGHT IN WEAKNESSES, IN INSULTS, IN HARDSHIPS, IN PERSECUTIONS, IN DIFFICULTIES. FOR WHEN I AM WEAK, THEN I AM STRONG. 2 CORINTHIANS 12:9-10, NIV

The events of Tuesday, September 11, 2001, completely reframed America's collective national consciousness. Americans are going to think and feel differently from now on. We lost two times the number of lives that we did on Pearl Harbor day. We lost a collective sense of security that may never be regained. As one newspaper put it, "America the invincible became America the vulnerable." But what did our losses evoke in our citizens and in our people?

First, we have been reminded of the fragility of life. Deep inside all of us, there's a subconscious awareness that our lives are quite precarious. We know disease can strike and accidents can happen; unforeseen events can interrupt our carefully planned lives. We do everything in our power to reduce that possibility, and in an affluent, peaceful society, we often convince ourselves that we are insulated from the bad things that happen to other people. When we live calamity-free for long periods of time, we slowly begin to take life itself for granted. We stop thanking God for sunrises and sunsets and for spring rains and fall colors. In a way we get too accustomed to the privilege of living—until a day like September 11 comes.

Life is relatively brief against the backdrop of eternity. It's a scandalously gracious gift from the hand of a good God, a gift that should be sincerely celebrated each day by those of us whose hourglasses still contain some grains of sand. Did you notice what people said in all those cell phone calls they made in the final moments of their lives from hijacked airplanes and burning buildings? They just said, "I love you. I love you. Tell Dad. Tell Mom. Tell the kids." We need to guard against growing complacent with our spouses and kids and parents and friends and colleagues and fellow church members. We need to be thankful for the gift of life.

There's a second reminder in the events of September 11: evil is alive and well. When times are peaceful and crime rates are falling and circumstances have been kind to us, we sometimes get lulled into forgetting that there's a ferocious battle being fought in this cosmos—a battle between the forces of good and evil. The Bible teaches from cover to cover that this spiritual war between the forces of good and evil is real. It's not folklore. It's not some religious fantasy. It's real. This battle is fought on the battlefields of individuals' minds and hearts. And the outcome of this battle will have an enormous impact on society.

A third lesson from this national nightmare pertains to a spiritual principle that's particularly difficult for American Christians to embrace. I sometimes call it the "winning-through-losing principle." It pertains to how God manages to produce something good out of the most difficult circumstances. I want to be very clear about this: no thinking person could attribute the actions of September 11 to the hand of a good God. God did not author what happened that Tuesday. God was repulsed by it. But in the middle of this horrendous catastrophe, God moved into action in curious, behind-the-scenes ways.

What has God been raising up out of the rubble on the eastern seaboard? First, we've seen unforgettable acts of heroism. I will never look at a firefighter the same way again. The hundreds of firefighters who ran toward the burning inferno instead of away from it—who ran up the steps of the World Trade Center while people were racing for their lives coming down—were stirred to do something that defies human logic. Their bravery becomes part of our collective national legacy. It dignifies all of us. The same can be said of police officers and other rescue workers. And then there were the airplane passengers who stormed the cockpit, where the hijackers were, driving the plane into the ground, to their own deaths, in order to avert a greater tragedy. These acts ennoble a nation.

Our loss also evoked an outpouring of volunteerism that takes one's breath away. Doctors drove hundreds of miles from their own high-paying jobs to go to New York City to serve, without pay, wherever they could be used. People opened their homes, offering food and refreshments to hundreds of rescue workers. Construction workers left their job sites, driving great distances with their own equipment in tow to help with the rescue efforts. So many willing volunteers showed up in downtown New York that rescue officials had to fence them out. People gave so much blood that the blood banks couldn't handle it all. I don't know that I've ever seen such an outpouring of volunteerism. And this is not the result of some great victory; it comes on the heels of a horrendous defeat. What is it—*who* is it—that stirs up such heroism and volunteerism during these times of terrible loss? I argue that it is God, working at his best against this terrible calamity.

And have you ever seen greater displays of unity in our land? Republicans and Democrats, arm-in-arm, singing together on the Capitol steps. Government agencies cooperating with each other. Flags waving from buildings and homes and cars. Some cynics say it's just emotion-driven patriotism and will be short-lived. I disagree. I think this is the result of our relentlessly redemptive God working behind the scenes, raising something good out of the rubble.

On top of all this, we are also seeing a return to our spiritual core. Against the backdrop of this horrendous loss, God has been using this catastrophe to remind us all that we need his help. We need his wisdom. We need his love, his assurance, his guidance, his strength. Churches have been jammed since September 11. The whole nation watched a church service on Friday, September 14. Again I remind you: a victory didn't produce this—a defeat did. And here is God, producing wonderful new things out of rubble heaps and broken lives.

What I've seen since September 11 has given me great hope for our country. I think we're learning the kinds of lessons from this national nightmare that will serve us for a long, long time. We are relearning that life is precious and that it needs to be celebrated. We're relearning that evil is alive and well and that we all need a strength and wisdom beyond our own to overcome it. We're relearning that ordinary people can still act heroically and courageously in difficult situations. We're relearning that volunteerism beats complacency and isolationism and an independent spirit, that unity is to be preferred over bickering and sniping. And we're relearning that a deep and abiding faith in God is the only foundation upon which the dream of our forefathers can be lived out. Amazingly, something really good is coming out of the rubble.

Only our relentlessly redemptive God could do this

quality of work. And now it's up to us to respond. If all of us will open ourselves up to the leadership and the love of God in a new way, something unbelievably redemptive will come out of this. And that is what I'm hoping and praying for.

 Our Father in heaven,
We look to you now to help us sort out our many
conflicted feelings and confusing emotions and to give
us your wisdom and your comfort for Christ's sake.
We look to you to work in our lives in these dark days. Speak to us,
God; we are listening. Teach us, God; we are willing to learn.
Prompt us, God; we will obey. Tell us what to do, and we will do it.
Help us to trust you. Amen.

My Thoughts and Prayers

_____

_____

_____

_____

_____

_____

_____

_____

_____

_____

_____

_____

_____

_____

_____

_____

_____

_____

_____

_____

"GOD, WHERE WERE YOU?"

by Chuck Colson

WE KNOW THAT WE ARE CHILDREN OF GOD AND
THAT THE WORLD AROUND US IS UNDER THE POWER
AND CONTROL OF THE EVIL ONE. AND WE KNOW
THAT THE SON OF GOD HAS COME, AND HE HAS GIVEN
US UNDERSTANDING SO THAT WE CAN KNOW THE
TRUE GOD. AND NOW WE ARE IN GOD BECAUSE WE
ARE IN HIS SON, JESUS CHRIST. HE IS THE ONLY TRUE
GOD, AND HE IS ETERNAL LIFE.   1 JOHN 5:19-20

IN THIS WORLD YOU WILL HAVE TROUBLE. BUT
TAKE HEART! I HAVE OVERCOME THE WORLD.

JOHN 16:33, NIV

Recently I received a call from a Christian friend who
was deeply troubled. The husband of a woman to whom
she had been witnessing had been killed in the World
Trade Center attack. The woman called my friend and

demanded bitterly, "Where was your God that you've been telling me about?"

Everywhere people are raising the same question: How could a good God have allowed such massive evil? No question poses a greater stumbling block to Christian faith; no question is more difficult for Christians to answer. Yet the biblical worldview does give us a good answer.

The simple answer to why bad things happen to so-called good people is that God loved us so much that he made us free moral agents in his image. He designed creatures with the ability to make choices, to choose either good or evil. The original humans, Adam and Eve, exercised that choice and chose to disobey God. In doing so, they rejected God's good, thus creating sin and opening the door to evil and death.

What happened on September 11, 2001, was raw, naked evil committed by men who made evil choices. But it was something else as well: a consequence of the fact that there is sin in the world. God could erase the consequences of sin immediately. But then we'd no longer be free moral agents; we would be robots. For without consequences, there is no real choice. God cannot simultaneously offer us free choice and then compel one choice over another—which is what would happen if he stopped all evil.

Jesus himself was asked why bad things happen to good people. In Luke 13 we read that people asked Jesus if the Galileans who were killed while sacrificing at the temple in Jerusalem were worse sinners than anyone else. "No," Jesus answered. And then he added, "Unless you repent you will all likewise perish" (Luke 13:3, NKJV). Jesus then reinforced his point: Recently a tower in a nearby city had fallen; eighteen people had been crushed to death. Jesus said, "Do you think that they were worse offenders than all the others who dwelt in Jerusalem? I tell you, No; but unless you repent you will all likewise perish" (Luke 13:4-5, RSV).

This is one of the hard sayings of Jesus, but there's great truth in it. We are in no position to ask God why terrible things happen. We're only to seek forgiveness ourselves.

What happened in New York, Pennsylvania, and Washington, D.C., was one of the worst tragedies in American history. But God can bring good out of evil, and he often works through adversity. Since the terrorist attacks, we have seen the nation come together with greater unity than I've witnessed since Pearl Harbor. And the Sunday after the attack, my church was filled to capacity at all services—very unusual in Florida at that time of year. Churches all over the country were packed out; even those in England and other countries were full.

People may be angry at God, but they're also asking questions about the meaning of life and God's role in it. You and I need to be prepared to answer the questions of people in pain. Where was God when terror struck? He was with us—just as he always is. He gave us everything we needed to cope with this or any other evils: he gave us himself on the cross at Calvary.

Almighty God,
You have made all the peoples of the earth for
your glory, to serve you in freedom and in peace.
Give to the people of our country a zeal for justice
and the strength of forbearance, that we may use our liberty in
accordance with your gracious will, through Jesus Christ our
Lord. Amen.

My Thoughts and Prayers

_____

_____

_____

_____

_____

_____

_____

_____

_____

_____

_____

_____

_____

_____

_____

_____

_____

_____

_____

_____

_____

_____

_____

A Trustworthy God

by James Dobson

I WILL PROCLAIM THE NAME OF THE LORD.
  OH, PRAISE THE GREATNESS OF OUR GOD!
HE IS THE ROCK, HIS WORKS ARE PERFECT,
  AND ALL HIS WAYS ARE JUST.
A FAITHFUL GOD WHO DOES NO WRONG,
  UPRIGHT AND JUST IS HE.   DEUTERONOMY 32:3-4, NIV

WE ALSO REJOICE IN OUR SUFFERINGS, BECAUSE WE
KNOW THAT SUFFERING PRODUCES PERSEVERANCE;
PERSEVERANCE, CHARACTER; AND CHARACTER, HOPE.

ROMANS 5:3-4, NIV

*I*f you are suffering because of disillusionment or confusion, I am writing with you in mind. I know you are hurting. I understand the pain that engulfed you when your child died or your husband betrayed you or your beloved wife went to be with Jesus. You could not explain the devastating earthquake, or the fire, or the terrible

19

tornado, or the unseasonable rainstorm that ruined your crops. The insurance company said it was an "act of God." Yes. That's what hurt the most.

The natural reaction is to say, "Lord, is *this* the way you treat your own? I thought you cared for me, but I was wrong. I can't love a God like that." It is a tragic misunderstanding.

I'm reminded of a woman who called in 1991 to tell me that her twenty-eight-year-old son had been killed in the Persian Gulf War. He was in a helicopter that was shot down somewhere over Iraq. He was her only son and was a born-again Christian. Only a handful of the 600,000 United Nations troops in that war failed to come home alive, yet this God-fearing man was one of them. My heart aches for his grieving mother.

Scripture is replete with examples of this troubling human experience. Moses, for instance, in his appeals to Pharaoh for the release of the children of Israel, had good reason to feel God had pushed him out on a limb and abandoned him there. He reacted as you or I would under the circumstances. "O Lord, why have you brought trouble upon this people? Is this why you sent me?" (Exodus 5:22, NIV).

The great danger for people who have experienced this kind of tragedy is that Satan will use their pain to make them feel victimized by God. What a deadly trap that is! When a person begins to conclude that he or she is disliked or hated by the Almighty, demoralization is not far behind.

For the heartsick, bleeding soul out there today who is desperate for a word of encouragement, let me assure you that you can trust the Lord of heaven and earth. There is security and rest in the wisdom of the eternal God. The Lord can be trusted—even when he can't be tracked. Of this you can be certain: Jehovah, King of kings and Lord of lords, is not pacing the corridors of heaven in confusion over the problems in your life! He hung the worlds in space. He can handle the burdens that have weighed you down, and he cares about you deeply.

Our view of God is too small—his power and his wisdom cannot even be imagined by us mortals. He is not just "the man upstairs" or "the great chauffeur in the sky" or some kind of wizard who will do a dance for those who make the right noises.

If we truly understood the majesty of the Lord and

the depth of his love for us, we would certainly accept those times when he defies human logic and sensibilities. Indeed, that is what we must do. Expect confusing experiences to occur along the way. Welcome them as friends—as opportunities for your faith to grow. Hold fast to your faith, without which it is impossible to please him. Never let yourself succumb to the notion to that God has somehow betrayed you. Instead, store away your questions in a file under the heading "Things I Don't Understand," and leave them there—and be thankful that God does what is best for us whether or not it conforms to our wishes.

Dear Lord,
When the difficult times come—disappointments and failures, heartaches and discouragements—help us to hold fast to our faith. May such hardships not turn us away from you but lead us to acknowledge our dependence on you alone. Amen.

My Thoughts and Prayers

_____

_____

_____

James Dobson

_____

_____

_____

_____

_____

_____

_____

_____

_____

_____

_____

_____

Stillness in Upheaval
by Ken Gire

GOD IS OUR REFUGE AND STRENGTH,
   A VERY PRESENT HELP IN TROUBLE.
THEREFORE WE WILL NOT FEAR, THOUGH THE
      EARTH SHOULD CHANGE,
   AND THOUGH THE MOUNTAINS SLIP INTO THE
      HEART OF THE SEA;
THOUGH ITS WATERS ROAR AND FOAM,
   THOUGH THE MOUNTAINS QUAKE AT ITS
      SWELLING PRIDE.
THERE IS A RIVER WHOSE STREAMS MAKE GLAD THE
      CITY OF GOD,
   THE HOLY DWELLING PLACES OF THE MOST
      HIGH.
GOD IS IN THE MIDST OF HER, SHE WILL NOT BE
      MOVED;
   GOD WILL HELP HER WHEN MORNING DAWNS.
THE NATIONS MADE AN UPROAR,
   THE KINGDOMS TOTTERED;
HE RAISED HIS VOICE,

THE EARTH MELTED.
THE LORD OF HOSTS IS WITH US;
    THE GOD OF JACOB IS OUR STRONGHOLD.

COME, BEHOLD THE WORKS OF THE LORD,
    WHO HAS WROUGHT DESOLATIONS IN THE
        EARTH.
HE MAKES WARS TO CEASE TO THE ENDS OF THE
        EARTH;
    HE BREAKS THE BOW AND CUTS THE SPEAR IN
        TWO;
    HE BURNS THE CHARIOT WITH FIRE.
"CEASE STRIVING AND KNOW THAT I AM GOD;
    I WILL BE EXALTED AMONG THE NATIONS,
    I WILL BE EXALTED IN THE EARTH."
THE LORD OF HOSTS IS WITH US;
    THE GOD OF JACOB IS OUR STRONGHOLD.

PSALM 46:1-11, NASB

*T*he pictures from this psalm form a composite of how uncertain life is and how terrifying it can become. One minute an embassy building is a safe haven for those seeking asylum. The next minute a terrorist bomb reduces the embassy to rubble. One minute Jerusalem is a city of peace. The next minute its streets are filled with gunfire from

Israeli soldiers and their Palestinian neighbors. One minute Mount St. Helens stands as a sturdy silhouette against the Washington state skies. The next minute it explodes, ripping away half the mountain, laying 150 square miles of forest to waste, and blanketing the state with volcanic ash.

For you and me it may not be a natural disaster we fear but a moral one. It may not be a political collapse that worries us but an emotional one. It may not be a military battle that is scaring us but a marital one.

Surviving these upheavals often depends on very basic things. When my wife and I used to live along the webwork of fault lines intersecting southern California, we were exposed to a lot of earthquake survival procedures. One of those procedures was to stay still. Most injuries, we were told, didn't come from the earthquake itself but occurred as people tried to escape the earthquake. As they scrambled out of the buildings they were in, many slipped and fell; others were hit by flying glass or falling debris. Some, in their panic, suffered heart attacks. The advice of professionals is to stay calm and be still.

That is also the advice of Psalm 46: "Cease striving." The original Hebrew word means to relax, to let the hand release its grip, to let the body go slack, to be still.

In his book of Sabbath poems, titled *A Timbered Choir,*
Wendell Berry describes what happens when we are still:

The mind that comes to rest is tended
In ways that it cannot intend:
Is borne, preserved, and comprehended
By what it cannot comprehend.

Poets know the importance of this kind of stillness. All
artists know it. They know that if they are still enough,
long enough, the art they are working on will speak to
them, will tell them what it wants to be and what it needs
from them to become it. All artists know this, whether
they work with paint or clay, words or musical notes.

Michelangelo knew how to be still before the stone
and listen to the David within it. Strauss knew how to be
still before the Danube and listen to the waltz eddying
about in its waters. Monet knew how to be still before the
pond and listen to the lilies sunning on its surface.

What we are asked to listen to in times of upheaval is
the voice of the Great Artist himself, who will one day
bring out of the upheavals in this world a new heaven and
a new earth. This Great Artist is also in the process of

bringing out of the upheavals in our lives a new heaven and new earth within us. Our culture knows little of this kind of listening. Unfortunately, the same is true of our religious culture.

In his book *The Pursuit of God,* A. W. Tozer wrote:

Religion has accepted the monstrous heresy that noise, size, activity, and bluster make a man dear to God. But we may take heart. To a people caught in the tempest of the last great conflict, God says, "Be still, and know that I am God" (Psalm 46:10, NIV), and still he says it, as if he means to tell us that our strength and safety lie not in noise but in silence.

Again, the insight of poet Wendell Berry:

Best of any song
is bird song
in the quiet, but first
you must have the quiet.

Best of any voice is the voice of God, especially in times of upheaval. But other voices clamor for our attention in times like these. Inner voices, mostly. Voices of denial, doubt, disillusionment, and despair. Voices that are anxious and fearful, anguished and regretful. Loud and insistent voices that drown out the voice of God. Consider these words from Henry Wadsworth Longfellow:

> *Let us then labour for an inward stillness,*
> *An inward stillness and an inward healing,*
> *That perfect silence where the lips and heart are still,*
> *And we no longer entertain our own imperfect*
> *Thought and vain opinions,*
> *But God above speaks in us,*
> *And we wait in singleness of heart,*
> *That we may know His will,*
> *And in the silence of our spirit*
> *That we may do His will,*
> *And do that only.*

Dear Lord,
Help us to be still and know that you are God. Speak to us in the stillness, Lord. We are waiting. We are listening. Amen.

My Thoughts and Prayers

_____

_____

_____

_____

_____

_____

_____

_____

_____

_____

_____

_____

_____

_____

_____

_____

_____

_____

_____

_____

_____

_____

_____

_____

_____

This photograph was taken by Skip Heitzig of the wreckage of the collapsed World Trade Center. Some would contend that the cross, formed when the massive metal support beams crashed to "Ground Zero," is merely an accident of physics. Others see a symbol placed by divine intent. Regardless of its origin, this cross reminds us of the sacrifice of Jesus Christ, who gave his life on another cross two thousand years ago to pay for our sins.

THE CROSS AT "GROUND ZERO"

by Skip Heitzig

AS FOR ME, GOD FORBID THAT I SHOULD BOAST
ABOUT ANYTHING EXCEPT THE CROSS OF OUR LORD
JESUS CHRIST.   GALATIANS 6:14

*T*he air was thick from the pulverized cement of the fallen
towers of the World Trade Center as the fireman pointed
to a cross. It hadn't been placed there by any person. It
was formed by massive metal support beams violently
ripped apart—a product of destruction. Yet there it
stood, a stark reminder of another death. The huge
fireman who showed it to me was adamant. "It was a sign!
I was pulling corpses out of this debris. No signs of life!
No hope! Then I looked up, and there it was!"

Five of us stood there studying it—two FBI agents, a
local police officer, the fireman, and me. In this solemn

place of mass murder and senseless death stood a reminder of the One who came to bring eternal life. Such a moment couldn't be more poignant. What's more, this same fireman who showed us the cross was determined to remove and preserve it as a memorial. We all locked arms, bowed our heads, and prayed—can you imagine? Three law enforcement professionals, a rescue worker, and a preacher praying that the cross and the One who gave his life on it two thousand years ago would not be forgotten—even here at "ground zero"!

"Ground zero" can come in many ways—not just the sudden crash of fuel-laden aircraft that turn buildings into rubble. It can be the sudden intrusion of an aggressive and fatal disease. For some it may come when a husband walks out, leaving a single mother to raise her children alone. It can strike when we least expect it—a fall from a ladder that renders its victim a quadriplegic. These experiences can reduce a life to ashes. It is at such times we need to see the cross. Why? Because the cross reminds us of a basic truth about suffering—the very worst thing can yield some of the very best things. God proved that himself! The greatest tragedy of human history was the death of God on a cross. Nothing could be more heinous. Yet it became the very best thing—now heaven's doors could be freely opened to the humans God created. Out of his death came our life. No wonder Paul made such a big deal about the Cross; he *boasted* in it. You should too—especially when you find your life reduced to the rubble of "ground zero." It could be the very place you find God more vividly than ever before.

Dear Lord,
We pray with the words of Isaac Watts:

Forbid it, Lord, that I should boast,
Save in the death of Christ, my God;
All the vain things that charm me most—
I sacrifice them to his blood.

Were the whole realm of nature mine,
That were a present far too small;
Love so amazing, so divine,
Demands my soul, my life, my all.

My Thoughts and Prayers

_____

_____

_____

THE LORD WHO
HEALS US

by Beth Moore

THEN MOSES LED THE PEOPLE OF ISRAEL AWAY FROM
THE RED SEA, AND THEY MOVED OUT INTO THE SHUR
DESERT. THEY TRAVELED IN THIS DESERT FOR THREE
DAYS WITHOUT WATER. WHEN THEY CAME TO
MARAH, THEY FINALLY FOUND WATER. BUT THE
PEOPLE COULDN'T DRINK IT BECAUSE IT WAS BITTER.
(THAT IS WHY THE PLACE WAS CALLED MARAH,
WHICH MEANS "BITTER.")   EXODUS 15:22-23

For several centuries our nation has been like the people
of Israel released from the bondage of Egypt. Like them,
our forefathers crossed the sea to worship their God in
liberty. No, the waters didn't part, but sometimes the
greater miracle is experiencing the victory when they
don't, when you feel the terror of the tempest and none-
theless choose to cross by faith. The disciples would never

have seen Jesus walking on the water had he simply parted the sea for them. But in the tossing of the waves, they saw his glory as he left footprints on the water.

For over two hundred years we've celebrated our deliverance much like the children of Israel in Exodus 15. They danced and sang, "I will sing to the Lord, for He is highly exalted. The horse and its rider He has hurled into the sea" (Exodus 15:1, NASB). As the years passed, we grew less and less aware of the One who delivered us for the express purpose of worship. Still, his patient hand has been upon us. We have been a mighty nation. No matter how we may have kidded ourselves otherwise, our strength has not come from our horses or chariots but from the outstretched arm of the Lord our God. He has been with us. And he is still with us even as he has allowed us to see the vulnerability of our forgetfulness.

Like the children of Israel, we stand at the bitter waters of Marah. Some of us stand on the shore and mourn for those who mourn. Others of us are waist-deep in the waters of personal tragedy and inexpressible loss. Like a mother who lost both husband and son. Like a husband who lost both wife and unborn child. Like a fiancée who waited for her groom to emerge from the ashes because their wedding date was a few short weeks away and she didn't want him to be late. We stand at the waters of Marah. The taste is bitter. And we are so tempted to drink.

No foe can defile us like bitterness. Its roots push their way through the most determined ground. Bitterness is one of the only states of the human soul that the Bible promises will cause much trouble and *defile many*. How do we defend ourselves against it? Hebrews 12:15 says, "See to it that no one misses the grace of God and that no bitter root grows up to cause trouble and defile many" (NIV). We must not miss the grace of God. It is there for us, whether we stand on the shore of Marah or whether, like some of those in New York City and Washington, D.C., we feel as though we are drowning underneath its toxic waters.

The grace of God doesn't come in prepackaged, one-size-fits-all containers. His grace is given according to our need. His mercies are new every morning. They belong to us by the cross of Christ. Oh, that we would allow God to plunge the wood of the cross into our bitter waters so that one day—*one day*—the waters will be sweet. Oh, that our pools of tears would become springs of revival.

God made a profound promise to his children in

Exodus 15:26. If they would just listen to him and do what was right, they would not take on the diseases of the Egyptians. Our enemy is not the Egyptians. Our enemy is terror. And he is diseased with hatred, scorn, violence, and an insatiable thirst for blood. Oh, that we would not catch his diseases. The most profound threat is not that we might catch the diseases the terrorists flew over this country to bring us. The most profound threats are the insidious diseases sent to attack both heart and soul. *That* is what we must defend ourselves against.

The grace not to become bitter—no matter what lies ahead—is ours if we want it. Crises invariably cause preoccupation. We cannot continue on with business as usual. We are changed. We must mourn. We must think. To be untouched right now could only mean that we are pitifully out of touch—with our own emotions, with our fellow creatures. These are days of preoccupation. We cannot help it. But we can decide where to direct our preoccupation. If we focus on our enemies, we will undoubtedly catch their diseases. But if we fix our gaze on God, if we incline our ear to his voice and do what is right even when what we feel is wrong, we will be healed. That is a promise. For he is the Lord who heals us.

O God our Healer,
Many are engulfed by the waters of Marah. They are
bitter, Lord. So bitter. Burning the throat. Poisoning
the heart. Marring the soul. Come, sweet Jesus. Show
your glory. Leave your prints on the waters. Plunge your cross in the
flood. And make the waters sweet before we drown. Amen.

My Thoughts and Prayers

PULLING UP
TO THE TABLE

by Jim Cymbala

THE REASON YOU DON'T HAVE WHAT YOU WANT IS
THAT YOU DON'T ASK GOD FOR IT.   JAMES 4:2

THE EARNEST PRAYER OF A RIGHTEOUS PERSON
HAS GREAT POWER AND WONDERFUL RESULTS.

JAMES 5:16

I am well aware that we don't get everything we ask
for; we have to ask according to God's will. But let us
not use theological dodges to avoid the fact that we often
go without things God wants us to have right now,
today, because we fail to ask. Too seldom do we get
honest enough to admit, "Lord, I can't handle this alone.
I've just hit the wall for the thirty-second time, and I
need you."

The words of the old hymn ring true:

Oh, what peace we often forfeit,
Oh, what needless pain we bear,
All because we do not carry
Everything to God in prayer.

God has chosen prayer as his channel of blessing. He has spread a table for us with every kind of wisdom, grace, and strength because he knows exactly what we need. But the only way we can get it is to pull up to the table and taste and see that the Lord is good.

Pulling up to the table is called the prayer of faith.

In other words, God doesn't tell us to pray because he wants to impose some sort of regimen on us. His is not a system of legalism. E. M. Bounds wrote, "Prayer ought to enter into the spiritual habits, but it ceases to be prayer when it is carried on by habit only. . . . Desire gives fervor to prayer. The soul cannot be listless when some great desire fixes and inflames it. . . . Strong desires make strong prayers."

The neglect of prayer is the fearful token of dead spiritual desires. The soul has turned away from God when desire after him no longer presses it into prayer. There can be no true praying without desire.

God says to us, "Pray, because I have all kinds of things for you, and when you ask, you will receive. I have all this grace, and you live with scarcity. Come unto me, all you who labor. Why are you so rushed? Where are you running now? Everything you need, I have."

If the times are indeed as bad as they seem . . . if the darkness in our world is growing heavier by the moment . . . if we are facing spiritual battles right in our own homes and churches . . . then we are foolish not to turn to the One who supplies unlimited grace and power. He is our only source.

The writer to the Hebrews nails down the most central activity of all for Christians in this verse: "Let us then approach the throne of grace with confidence, so that we may receive mercy and find grace to help us in our time of need" (Hebrews 4:16, NIV). This is where we encounter God, the only One powerful and loving enough to change our lives.

Almighty God,
What a staggering concept this is— that we frail and
fallen human beings can come directly to the throne
of the Creator of the universe. And we come not
fearfully, crawling and apologetic, but with confidence that we will

receive your mercy and grace. How foolish we are to neglect this privilege. We open our hearts to your Spirit, asking you to prompt us to pray without ceasing. Amen.

My Thoughts and Prayers

_____

_____

_____

_____

_____

_____

_____

_____

_____

_____

_____

_____

_____

_____

_____

_____

_____

GOD'S SILENCE,
OUR QUESTIONS

by Max Lucado

AFTER JESUS FINISHED TELLING THESE THINGS TO HIS
TWELVE FOLLOWERS, HE LEFT THERE AND WENT TO
THE TOWNS IN GALILEE TO TEACH AND PREACH.

JOHN THE BAPTIST WAS IN PRISON, BUT HE HEARD
ABOUT WHAT CHRIST WAS DOING. SO JOHN SENT
SOME OF HIS FOLLOWERS TO JESUS. THEY ASKED HIM,
"ARE YOU THE ONE WHO IS TO COME, OR SHOULD WE
WAIT FOR SOMEONE ELSE?"   MATTHEW 11:1-3, NCV

*H*e was a child of the desert. Leathery face. Tanned skin.
Clothing of animal skins. What he owned fit in a pouch.
His walls were the mountains, and his ceiling, the stars.

But not anymore. His frontier is walled out, his hori-
zon hidden. The stars are memories. The fresh air is all but
forgotten. And the stench of the dungeon relentlessly

reminds this child of the desert that he is now a captive of the king.

In anyone's book, John the Baptist deserves better treatment than this. After all, isn't he the forerunner of the Christ? Isn't he a relative of the Messiah? At the very least, isn't his the courageous voice of repentance? Is this how God rewards his anointed? Is this how he honors his faithful? Is this how God crowns his chosen—with a dark dungeon and the threat of a shiny blade? The inconsistency was more than John could take.

Even before Herod reached his verdict, John was asking his questions. When he had a chance to get a message to Jesus, his inquiry was one of despair: "Are you really the Messiah we've been waiting for, or should we keep looking for someone else?" Had the Bible been written by a public-relations agency, they would have eliminated that verse. It's not good PR strategy to admit that one of the cabinet members has doubts about the president. You don't let stories like that get out if you are trying to present a unified front.

But the Scriptures weren't written by PR agents; they were inspired by an eternal God who knew that every disciple from then on would spend time in the dungeon of doubt. Although the circumstances have changed, the questions haven't. They are asked anytime the faithful suffer the consequences of the faithless. Anytime a person takes a step in the right direction only to have her feet knocked out from under her; anytime a person does a good deed but suffers evil results; anytime a person takes a stand only to end up flat on his face . . . the questions fall like rain. *If God is so good, why do I hurt so badly? If God is really there, why am I here? What did I do to deserve this? Did God slip up this time? Why are the righteous persecuted? Does God sometimes sit on his hands? Does God sometimes choose to do nothing? Does God sometimes opt for silence even when I'm screaming my loudest?*

John couldn't believe that anything less than his release would be for the best interest of all involved. In his opinion it was time to exercise some justice and get some action. But the One who had the power was "sitting on his hands." If you've heard the silence of God, if you've been left standing in the dungeon of doubt, then understand this: Perhaps it isn't that God is silent. Perhaps, like John, you've been listening for the wrong answer. John had been listening for an answer to his earthly problems, while Jesus was busy resolving his heavenly ones. That's worth remembering the next time you hear the silence of God.

The fact is, John wasn't asking too much; he was asking too little. He was asking the Father to resolve the temporary, while Jesus was busy resolving the eternal. John was asking for immediate favor, while Jesus was orchestrating the eternal solution. Does that mean that Jesus has no regard for injustice? No. He cares about persecutions. He cares about inequities and hunger and prejudice. And he knows what it is like to be punished for something he didn't do. He knows the meaning of the phrase "It's just not right." For while Jesus was on the cross, God did sit on his hands. He did turn his back. He did ignore the screams of the innocent. He sat in silence while the sins of the world were placed upon his Son. And he did nothing while a cry a million times bloodier than John's echoed in the black sky: "My God, my God, why have you forsaken me?" (Matthew 27:46). Was it right? No. Was it fair? No. Was it love? Yes. In a world of injustice, God once and for all tipped the scales in the favor of hope. And he did it by sitting on his hands so that we could know the kingdom of God.

Dear Lord,

We want more than anything else to see you and know you. Please, Lord, help us to truly believe. Thank you that you are real and that you care deeply about us. We know that you see our hearts and our thoughts. Help us to know whether we are looking in the wrong direction to find you; if we are, please direct our eyes toward you. Help us to remember that you hold the eternal perspective and that even when we don't understand your methods, you are working in our lives. Amen.

My Thoughts and Prayers

_____

_____

_____

_____

_____

_____

_____

_____

_____

_____

_____

_____

_____

Overcoming Evil
with Good

by Chuck Colson

DO NOT REPAY ANYONE EVIL FOR EVIL. BE CAREFUL
TO DO WHAT IS RIGHT IN THE EYES OF EVERYBODY. IF
IT IS POSSIBLE, AS FAR AS IT DEPENDS ON YOU, LIVE AT
PEACE WITH EVERYONE. DO NOT TAKE REVENGE, MY
FRIENDS, BUT LEAVE ROOM FOR GOD'S WRATH, FOR
IT IS WRITTEN: "IT IS MINE TO AVENGE; I WILL REPAY,"
SAYS THE LORD. ON THE CONTRARY: "IF YOUR ENEMY
IS HUNGRY, FEED HIM; IF HE IS THIRSTY, GIVE HIM
SOMETHING TO DRINK. IN DOING THIS, YOU WILL
HEAP BURNING COALS ON HIS HEAD." DO NOT BE
OVERCOME BY EVIL, BUT OVERCOME EVIL WITH
GOOD.   ROMANS 12:17-21, NIV

*T*he terrorist attacks that destroyed the World Trade
Center in New York and damaged the Pentagon were not
just about buildings and airplanes. They were about

people. People who survived and people who died. The country grieves. In the midst of this, Christians are called to be, as Augustine put it, "the best of citizens." But what should we be doing?

Practically speaking, we can do such things as donating time or money to the relief effort. But just as important, we can listen. The magnitude of these terrorist attacks cuts to the heart and soul of many American communities as our neighbors lost friends or loved ones in airplanes and buildings. Beyond that, many Americans, including our children, have been glued to the television, watching events as they unfold. People are traumatized and confused. They need to talk, and we can listen and give a reason for our hope.

We can also be an influence on those around us. For example, we can love our Muslim and Middle Eastern neighbors. Our instinct for self-preservation may cause us to see someone in traditional Muslim dress or with Arabic features and wonder if he or she represents a threat. At the same time, we know that most Arabs living in America are Christians—Christians who have fled from the kind of militant Islamic leaders who were behind the terror of September 11. Beyond that, the vast majority of Muslims living in the United States are peaceful and law-abiding people. Christians should be the first to recognize this and befriend those who will find themselves shunned by many.

Most important, we need to pray. Pray fervently for our leaders. Enormous wisdom—nothing less than God's wisdom—is required. Paul wrote to the Romans, "Overcome evil with good" (Romans 12:21, NIV). One of the reasons I believe the Christian gospel couldn't be a made-up religion, as some people think, is that it tells us to do that which is contrary to our human nature. When evil is done to us, the human instinct is to respond with evil. The result is that evil triumphs. In this case, if we responded to the terrorist attacks with evil, the terrorists would win. But the Bible tells us to act exactly contrary to our own nature, to respond to evil with good.

The most powerful example of this principle I know is Friar Jerzy Popieluszko, a Catholic priest in Poland in the early 1980s. The pale, gaunt priest had a twofold message: Defend the truth, and overcome evil with good. People responded and overflowed his church. The secret police followed him everywhere. He began to receive threats until one night, after celebrating Mass and preaching, Friar Jerzy disappeared.

About ten days later, as fifty thousand people came to Mass and to listen to a tape of the priest's last sermon, they heard that his body had been found in the Vistula River—badly mutilated by torture. The secret police braced for an uprising. But on the day of Friar Jerzy's funeral, the huge crowd that walked past their headquarters bore a banner and shouted what it said: "We forgive." Friar Jerzy had taught them well.

Only Christians, men and women who are touched by and understand the present reality of the Cross, can possibly overcome evil with good. And if we don't, no one else will. Rage and anger will carry the day, and the terrorists will have won.

This doesn't obviate the government's use of the sword—military force—to swiftly and proportionately respond to terrorist attacks. We must do that, and our government has. But as the nation's anger rises, there is a great test for American Christians: Can we live by the gospel? Will we love our neighbors—even those who look, sound, or seem like those who so ruthlessly attacked us? This is a time when our anger must be tempered with patience and restraint. May God have mercy on us.

Dear Lord,
It is natural for us to feel anger. It is natural for us
to want revenge. Yet your gospel teaches us to
respond to evil in a way that is not natural but
supernatural. Empower us with your Holy Spirit, that we may,
as instructed in your Word, overcome evil with good. Amen.

My Thoughts and Prayers

_____

_____

_____

_____

_____

_____

_____

_____

_____

_____

_____

_____

_____

_____

FORGIVE YOUR ENEMIES

Kenneth N. Taylor

IF YOU FORGIVE THOSE WHO SIN AGAINST YOU, YOUR
HEAVENLY FATHER WILL FORGIVE YOU. BUT IF YOU
REFUSE TO FORGIVE OTHERS, YOUR FATHER WILL
NOT FORGIVE YOUR SINS.   MATTHEW 6:9-13

THEN PETER CAME TO HIM AND ASKED, "LORD, HOW
OFTEN SHOULD I FORGIVE SOMEONE WHO SINS
AGAINST ME? SEVEN TIMES?"

"NO!" JESUS REPLIED, "SEVENTY TIMES SEVEN!"
                                    MATTHEW 18:21-22

*O*n the morning of September 11, I was awakened by a
shout from my brother-in-law, who was watching the
morning news. I joined him, and before our eyes, the
great twin towers of the World Trade Center collapsed
into billowing heaps, entombing thousands of people. The
Pentagon, that symbolic fortress of our national strength,

was pierced and left crippled and smoking. Then we heard the news of a hijacked plane crashing in the grain fields of rural Pennsylvania, apparently headed toward our nation's capital. Christian brothers and sisters, people of other faiths, visitors to our country, and our own citizens—office workers, police officers, firefighters, and rescue workers—died alongside all the passengers and crews of those four hijacked planes.

Our nation finds itself in a quandary unlike any in its history. As a country, we have been wounded, and our senses of freedom and invulnerability have been violated. But ours is not a conventional foe. Those who attacked our nation do not fear death; they rejoice in it. They do not cherish freedom; they hate it. They do not attack our nation's military forces; they deliberately attack its civilians—its men and women and children.

As a mighty nation, we may have the power and ability to rectify these injustices. Discerning right from wrong in the use of that power, however, is difficult—especially with so many more human lives on the line. Will we bomb to rubble those rural nations whose leaders helped perpetrate the horrible events of

September 11? Will we be responsible for punishing innocent civilians along with their despotic rulers? Are there individuals and groups who lurk in the shadows, awaiting their opportunity to attack our nation again? What form will the next attack take? These are the just a few of the questions facing our president and our country.

Our nation's leaders aren't the only ones asking questions—each one of us has been affected by the tragic events of that September morning. Even now, we find the events difficult to comprehend; navigating the waters between a desire for revenge and the responsibility to forgive seems impossible. In this situation we are given two instructions by God—one far easier to accept than the other.

First, we are to pray. God says, "If my people who are called by my name will humble themselves and pray and seek my face and turn from their wicked ways, I will hear from heaven and will forgive their sins and heal their land" (2 Chronicles 7:14). In the New Testament we are reminded, "The earnest prayer of a righteous person has great power and wonderful results" (James 5:16). Pray for wisdom for our leaders. Pray for comfort for those families who are mourning. Pray, too, for the people in and around Afghanistan—the poor, the uneducated, and the victims of oppressive leadership. Pray that our nation's actions will lead to a godly and peaceful life for all. Morning, noon, and night we should pray.

Second, we are to forgive our enemies. Jesus said, "Love your enemies. Do good to those who hate you. . . . Pray for those who hurt you" (Luke 6:27-28). *Even in the face of such cruelty and devastation? Even though my family is wounded and my heart is breaking?* Yes, it is a command of the Lord. What we often pray so easily on Sunday mornings is now a challenge to us: "Forgive us our sins, just as we have forgiven those who have sinned against us" (Matthew 6:12). We need the Lord's help to do this.

My prayer is that each of us will be ready and willing to do whatever is asked of us. To endure. To give. To pray. Yes, even to forgive. My prayer for myself and my country and God's church is that each of us will be ready to obey the Lord's commands.

Kenneth N. Taylor

Dear Lord,
Be with us in this time of fear and uncertainty. Give
wisdom to our president and the nation's leaders.
Comfort those who are grieving and inconsolable.
Help us to be ready to do whatever it is you ask us to do. Let us be
open to your will for our lives. Give us the strength to forgive. In
Jesus' name, amen.

My Thoughts and Prayers

_____

_____

_____

_____

_____

_____

_____

_____

_____

_____

_____

_____

WHILE WE WERE YET SINNERS

by *Walter Wangerin*

As they were eating, Jesus took a loaf of bread and asked God's blessing on it. Then he broke it in pieces and gave it to the disciples, saying, "Take it, for this is my body."

And he took a cup of wine and gave thanks to God for it. He gave it to them, and they all drank from it. And he said to them, "This is my blood, poured out for many, sealing the covenant between God and his people. I solemnly declare that I will not drink wine again until that day when I drink it new in the Kingdom of God."

MARK 14:22-25

When is a mother more inclined to cuddle her children? When they're a nasty, insolent brood, disobedient and disrespectful of her motherhood? Or when they are cuddly?

When will a father most likely give good gifts to his children? When they've just ruined the previous gift by negligence or by downright wickedness? When they are sullen and self-absorbed? Or when they manifest genuine goodness and self-responsibility?

But the love of Jesus is utterly unaccountable—except that he is God, and God is love. It has no cause in us. It reacts to, or repays, or rewards nothing in us. It is beyond human measure, beyond human comprehension. It takes my breath away.

For when did Jesus choose to give us the supernatural, enduring gift of his presence, his cuddling, his dear communing with us? When we were worthy of the gift, good people indeed? Hardly. It was precisely when we were most unworthy. When our wickedness was directed particularly at him.

It was to the insolent and the hateful that he gave his gift of personal love.

In 1 Corinthians 11, the apostle Paul describes the scene of the Last Supper, when Jesus Christ represented his coming self-sacrifice by serving his disciples bread, symbolizing his broken body, and wine, symbolizing his spilled blood. Paul writes, "The Lord Jesus, the same night in which he was betrayed, took bread" (1 Corinthians 11:23, NKJV). Oh, let us read those words, *the same night,* with awe. For who among us can hear them just before receiving the gift of Christ's intimacy and not be overcome with wonder, stunned at such astonishing love? The context qualifies that love. The time defines it. And over and over again these words remind us of the times: *the same night in which he was betrayed . . .*

"While we were still weak," says Paul, "at the right time Christ died for the ungodly" (Romans 5:6, RSV). Not for the godly and the good, but "while we were yet sinners Christ died for us" (Romans 5:8, RSV). Then! That same night! When absolutely nothing recommended us. When "we were enemies" (Romans 5:10, RSV). Enemies! In the night when his people betrayed him—the night of intensest enmity—the dear Lord Jesus said, "This is my blood of the covenant, which is poured out for many" (Mark 14:24, RSV). Then! Can we comprehend the joining of two such extremes, the good and the evil together? In the night of gravest human treachery, he gave the gift of himself. And the giving has never ceased. The holy Communion continues today.

But in that *same* night he remembered our need. In that *same* night he provided the sacrament that would forever contain his grace and touch his comfort into us.

Oh, this is a love past human expectation. This is beyond all human deserving. This, therefore, is a love so celestial that it shall endure long—longer than we do.

This is grace.

 Behold, Lord,
I am of small account. What shall I say to thee? I lay my hand upon my mouth. Your love is too wonderful for me! It is high; I can't understand it. But this I do: I dwell within it, silently, gratefully, faithfully, believing in it after all. Amen.

My Thoughts and Prayers

_____

_____

_____

_____

_____

_____

_____

_____

_____

_____

The Things That
Matter Most

by James Robison

I want you to share your food with the
hungry and to welcome poor wanderers into
your homes. Give clothes to those who need
them, and do not hide from relatives who need
your help.

If you do these things, your salvation will
come like the dawn. Yes, your healing will
come quickly. . . . Feed the hungry and help
those in trouble. Then your light will shine
out from the darkness, and the darkness
around you will be as bright as day.

Isaiah 58:7-8, 10

On the evening of September 11, 2001, America shifted
its focus to the *real* issues of life. In a matter of a few
hours, the things we once held in such high regard

suddenly found the right place in our lives—way down the ladder of importance. Our robust economy, which many Americans had placed above God, was shaken to the core. Spectators weren't interested in going to baseball games, and the athletes didn't want to play. Meetings and flights were canceled, and many businesses closed their doors.

Fortunately, in this time of crisis, people flocked to houses of worship to pray. Families cocooned in their homes to get the latest news. The nation rightly turned its attention to the rescue efforts and surrounding issues.

I suspect we will never be the same. And who wants to stay in the status quo? Surely every believer's heart cries for something good to come out of the bad. We desire to be more mindful and sensitive to the needs of those around us—and there are plenty of opportunities to put our love into action. We don't have to go very far to find people who need a friend to hold them, listen to them, shed tears with them, rejoice with them when something good comes their way.

In the aftermath of the recent American horror, people are beginning to see that one of the greatest aspects of life is *sharing* life. God wants us to release the river of his life and love and to lay aside meaningless discussions and arguments.

Remember the headlines you saw and heard before September 11? Today they seem trivial, don't they? I believe we are now focusing on what really matters: restored relationships, unity of spirit, and compassion for the suffering.

On the night of the horrific attacks, my wife, Betty, and I appeared on one of the Christian networks, and I was led to read Isaiah 58. In this chapter Isaiah admonishes us not to hide ourselves from those in need. He says to divide our bread with the hungry and to bring the homeless and poor into our homes. When we see the naked, we are to cover them. When we satisfy the desire of the afflicted, our efforts will not go unrewarded. God promises to "continually guide you"; he says, "Your light will rise in darkness, and your gloom will become like midday" (Isaiah 58:10-11, NASB).

I believe that what the enemy thought was the end was instead the beginning of a new day in American life. They tried to knock us down and, instead, they stood us up—and we will stand taller than we've ever stood before. America has been brought to attention. We need to refocus our vision and reestablish the age-old foundations. May we all be expressions of God's love and continue to focus on those things that matter most.

Dear Lord,
Help us, in the wake of tragedy, to focus on the things that really matter. Help us to be your hands and feet, showing compassion to all who suffer or who are in need. Amen.

My Thoughts and Prayers

James Robison

24-KARAT SAINTS

by Lenya Heitzig

I WILL BRING THE ONE-THIRD THROUGH THE FIRE,
WILL REFINE THEM AS SILVER IS REFINED,
AND TEST THEM AS GOLD IS TESTED.
THEY WILL CALL ON MY NAME,
AND I WILL ANSWER THEM.
I WILL SAY, "THIS IS MY PEOPLE";
AND EACH ONE WILL SAY, "THE LORD IS MY GOD."

ZECHARIAH 13:9, NKJV

Take comfort, weary one, with this thought: God carefully selects a precious few to be refined by the fire of affliction. Not every believer is ready for the test that fiery trials surely bring. In ancient Babylon, only Shadrach, Meshach, and Abednego were privileged enough to be thrown into the fiery furnace and there discover that "the Son of God" (Daniel 3:25, NKJV) would walk with them in the midst of the flames.

Those handpicked by God to go through the fire are made capable by him to endure the heat so that they may come forth as pure gold. The Savior is refining 24-karat saints: shining ones to reflect his image—so that of them he can say, "These are my people"—and sparkling ones to proclaim, "The Lord is my God."

Television personality Arthur Godfrey used to recount a lesson he learned while watching a local blacksmith separate scrap metal into two piles. After carefully examining each piece, the blacksmith cast some metal into a pile on his right while the other scraps were thrown into a heap on his left.

Godfrey asked the blacksmith what the two piles represented. The smithy replied, "I can see that some of that metal will be useful when it is put through the fire. There is something in it that will let it go through the fire and come out refined and perfected. But the other metal is useless—it cannot take the fire, so I have to toss it onto the junk heap."

That experience forged a favorite prayer that Godfrey uttered throughout his life. Whenever a difficult circumstance turned up the heat, he knew that God was using that fiery trial to refine him. Believing that God's ultimate goal was to make him a better man, a 24-karat saint, Arthur would pray, "Lord, the fire, not the junk heap!"

Has God divinely placed you in the midst of a situation that seems too hot to handle? Perhaps it was ignited by an unfaithful spouse, a rebellious child, an unrelenting illness, a financial loss, or an untimely death. Instead of asking God, "Why me?" your response should be, "Why not me?" If Jesus, God in human flesh, was refined by the furnace of affliction (see Revelation 1:14-15), then why not us? May we each find the courage to pray not for rescue from the fire but for the grace to come through it as pure as gold.

Dear Lord,
Let affliction come, for it reveals that God has chosen
me. Whatever form the flames may take, help me to
see the Son of God in the midst of them. Purify my
life until it shines like 24-karat gold, reflecting the Savior. Lord,
the fire, not the junk heap! Amen.

My Thoughts and Prayers

_____

_____

_____

_____

CONQUERING FEAR

by Philip Yancey

DO NOT FEAR ANYTHING EXCEPT THE LORD
ALMIGHTY. HE ALONE IS THE HOLY ONE. IF YOU
FEAR HIM, YOU NEED FEAR NOTHING ELSE.

ISAIAH 8:13

Fear is the universal primal response to suffering. And
yet beyond doubt it is also the single greatest enemy of
recovery.

English poet and clergyman John Donne knew fear
well. He wrote his meditations in a day when waves of
bubonic plague, the Black Death, were sweeping through
his city of London. The last epidemic alone had killed forty
thousand people. Thousands more fled to the countryside,
transforming whole neighborhoods into ghost towns. For
six weeks Donne lay at the threshold of death, believing he
had contracted the plague.

After noting signs of fear in his attending physician, Donne set down this description:

> Fear insinuates itself in every action or passion of the mind, and as gas in the body will counterfeit any disease, and seem the stone, and seem the gout, so fear will counterfeit any disease of the mind. . . . I know not what fear is, nor I know not what it is that I fear now; I fear not the hastening of my death, and yet I do fear the increase of the disease; I should belie nature if I should deny that I feared this.

People who are suffering, whether from physical or psychological pain, often feel an oppressive sense of aloneness. They feel abandoned, by God and also by others, because they must bear the pain alone and because no one else quite understands. Loneliness increases the fear, which in turn increases the pain, and downward the spiral goes.

At another level, the spiritual level, my study of the Bible has convinced me that the fact of suffering does not mean God is against me. Mainly through the example of Jesus, I have learned to see that God is on our side. Paul calls God, appropriately, "the Father of compassion and the God of all comfort" (2 Corinthians 1:3, NIV).

The Bible is the Christian's guidebook, and I believe its wisdom about suffering offers a great antidote to fear. "Perfect love drives out fear" (1 John 4:18, NIV). Personal knowledge of the God of perfect love can conquer fear as light destroys darkness. I need not engage in frenzied efforts to muster up faith. God is already full of loving concern, and I need not impress him with spiritual calisthenics.

The Christian has many resources available to help stave off fear; Donne's *Devotions,* in fact, offers a wonderful model of a Christian learning to disarm fear. Donne knew fear well. Most of the time he battled such fears alone, for in those days victims of contagious diseases were subject to quarantine. As he lay on his bed, he wondered if God, too, was participating in the quarantine. Where was God's promised presence?

Donne's real fear was not of the tinny clamor of pain all over his body; he feared God. He asked the "Why me?" question over and over again. He wondered if God was behind the plague after all. Guilt from his spotted past lurked like a demon nearby. Perhaps he was indeed suffering as a result of some previous sin.

Donne never really resolves the "Why me?" questions in his book, but *Devotions* does record, step by step, how he came to resolve his fears. Obsessed, he reviews every biblical occurrence of the word *fear*. As he does so, it dawns on him that life will always include circumstances that incite fear: if not illness, financial hardship; if not poverty, rejection; if not loneliness, failure. In such a world, Donne has a choice: to fear God, or to fear every-thing else.

Donne determines that his best course is to cultivate a proper fear of the Lord, for that fear can supplant all others. Finally he prays, "As thou hast given me a repen-tance, not to be repented of, so give me, O Lord, a fear, of which I may not be afraid." In the most important sense, it did not matter whether his sickness was a chas-tening or merely a natural accident. In either case he would trust God, for in the end trust represents the proper fear of the Lord.

Dear Lord,
When our circumstances fill us with fear, help us
to trust in you, remembering that your perfect
love casts out fear. Help us to feel your loving
arms around us. Amen.

My Thoughts and Prayers

_____

_____

_____

_____

_____

_____

_____

_____

_____

_____

_____

_____

_____

_____

_____

_____

_____

_____

_____

_____

When I Am Afraid

by Luci Swindoll

When I am afraid, I put my trust in you.

PSALM 56:3

$\mathscr{A}$ dear friend of mine who teaches elementary school music got a timely reminder recently of how much simpler life can be when God is in the picture. One Monday afternoon she was feeling apprehensive about having to change the date for a musical program on the school calendar. It meant she had to face the principal, ask for the change, and possibly have her request rejected. As you may know, one can't just arbitrarily switch dates of the orchestra concert and the big basketball game, for example. These events are determined months in advance and are generally set in concrete!

As she busied herself in her classroom, she rehearsed what she would say to the principal. The fear began to rise in her so much that her anxiety was out of proportion to her upcoming request. She had that "fretful" feeling. While dusting off her desk, she swept a small scrap of paper to the floor. When she picked it up, she was amazed to read the words "When I am afraid, I will trust in you." She could hardly believe her eyes; it was just the encouragement she needed to accomplish the task at hand.

She smiled to herself, took a deep breath, and walked straight to the principal's office for her talk. Everything worked out beautifully, and the date was changed on the calendar with only minor adjustments.

Several days later a little girl in one of her music classes came up to her and whispered, "Mrs. Jacobs, have you by any chance seen a piece of paper with the words 'When I am afraid, I will trust in you' written on it?" My friend told the child that she had seen the paper and that it was on her desk.

"Is it yours, Rachel?" The child told her it was. Wanting to make the most of the moment, my friend asked, "Are you all right, honey? How did you happen to have that piece of paper in the first place? Is there anything I can help you with?"

Rachel confided, "Well, remember a few days ago when we had to take all those tests? I was afraid I couldn't pass, so my mom put that note in my lunch box that day, and it really helped me. Then somehow I lost it."

My friend then explained how the child's loss was her gain. She expressed that she, too, had feared something, found the paper on the floor, and was reminded to face and overcome that fear by trusting God. The very thing that had calmed the heart of the little child was the same thing that calmed the heart of the wise and mature school-teacher.

Fear is indiscriminate. It affects all of us regardless of our age or position in life. Whether our fear is absolutely realistic or out of proportion in our minds, our greatest refuge is Jesus Christ.

You may wonder how to find that refuge. It is really very simple: As you walk through your days, you encounter various situations in life that trouble you. For me, there are decisions that must be made that seem bigger than I have the capacity to handle. Or there's a relationship in my life that's out of whack and needs attention. Perhaps it's a money problem or a doctor's dreaded report that has me upset.

At times like these we can quiver in our boots and become paralyzed by that "deer caught in the headlights" phenomenon, we can retreat completely, we can convince ourselves that the problem doesn't exist, or we can talk to the One who is able to calm our apprehensions and fears and give us courage to move ahead with a heart of confidence and assurance. In other words, we can pray.

There are times you might be so fearful that all you can say is, "Lord, I'm scared. Please give me peace because I'm placing my trust in you. I know you can meet me right here. Please do!" And he will. He will enter into your mind and calm you with his presence.

God wants us to know that he is with us; he is for us. That's why he has given us this verse. Write it out on a piece of paper today, and tuck it in your purse or pocket as a reminder that he is greater than your fear.

Dear Lord,
What a blessing it is to know you are my strength and my confidence. I am so glad I don't have to depend on myself at this moment. Give me the comfort I need to meet my fear head-on, knowing full well that I am completely safe when I put my trust in you. Amen.

My Thoughts and Prayers

_____

_____

_____

_____

_____

_____

_____

_____

_____

_____

_____

_____

_____

_____

_____

_____

_____

_____

_____

_____

_____

_____

_____

_____

_____

WHEN ALL THAT IS GOOD
FALLS APART

by Max Lucado

"WHEN ALL THAT IS GOOD FALLS APART,
WHAT CAN GOOD PEOPLE DO?"

THE LORD IS IN HIS HOLY TEMPLE;
the LORD SITS ON HIS THRONE IN HEAVEN.

PSALM 11:3-4, NCV

*I*sn't David's question ours? When all that is good falls apart, what can good people do? When planes pierce strong towers, when flames crown our fortress, when cities shake and people plunge, what are we to do?

In some ways the terrible events of September 11, 2001, are like an awful dream. We're still hoping we'll wake up. But we won't. For what we saw was not a dream.

It was unspeakable, unthinkable, but it was not a dream. People did perish. Buildings did fall.

And we are sad. We are sad for the innocent people who died, for their children who will not see them again, for spouses who must now live without them. We grieve the loss of life.

But our grief goes even deeper. As we mourn the death of people, we mourn the death of an image. Just as the skyline of New York City is forever altered, so is our view of the world. We thought we were untouchable, impenetrable. With the loss of innocent lives is the loss of innocence itself. Perhaps we should have known better, but we didn't.

So we ask with David, "When all that is good falls apart, what can good people do?" (Psalm 11:3, NCV). Curiously, David doesn't answer his question with an answer. He answers it with a declaration: "The Lord is in his holy temple; the Lord sits on his throne in heaven" (Psalm 11:4, NCV).

His point is unmistakable: God is unaffected by our storms. He is undeterred by our problems. He is unfrightened by these problems. He is in his holy temple. He is on his throne in heaven.

Buildings have fallen, but he has not. God has made a business out of turning tragedy into triumph.

Did he not do so with Joseph? Look at him in the Egyptian prison. His brothers have sold him out; Potiphar's wife has turned him in. If ever a world has caved in, Joseph's has.

Or consider Moses, watching flocks in the wilderness. Is this what he intended to do with his life? Hardly. His heart beats with Hebrew blood. His passion is to lead the slaves, so why does God have him leading sheep?

And what about Daniel? He was among the brightest and best young men of Israel, the equivalent of a West Point cadet or Ivy Leaguer. But he and his entire generation are marched out of Jerusalem. The city is destroyed. The temple is in ruins.

Joseph in prison. Moses in the desert. Daniel in chains. These were dark moments. Who could have seen any good in them? Who could have known that Joseph the prisoner was just one promotion away from becoming Joseph the prime minister? Who would have thought that God was giving Moses forty years of wilderness training in the very desert through which he would lead the people? And who could have imagined that Daniel the captive would soon be Daniel the king's counselor?

God does things like that. He did with Joseph, with Moses, with Daniel, and, most of all, he did with Jesus.

What we saw in September is what the followers of Christ saw on the cross. They saw innocence slaughtered, goodness murdered. Heaven's tower of strength was pierced. Mothers wept, evil danced, and the apostles had to wonder, *When all that is good falls apart, what can good people do?*

God answered their question with a declaration. With the rumble of the earth and the rolling of the rock he reminded them, "The Lord is in his holy temple; the Lord sits on his throne in heaven."

And, today, we must remember: he still is. He is still in his temple, still on his throne, still in control. And he still makes princes out of prisoners, counselors out of captives, and Sundays out of Fridays. What he did then, he will do still.

It falls to us to ask him to do so.

 Dear Lord,
When disaster strikes, we so easily become lost. We have no idea what to do. So we turn to you. Thank you that you are in your holy temple; thank you that you are on your throne in heaven. We know that you are in control; we acknowledge our dependence on you. Thank you for your strength, for your presence with us. Thank you that no

matter what happens, we can lean on you, resting in your arms
and relying on your steadfastness. Thank you for your
unconditional love for us. Amen.

My Thoughts and Prayers

_____

_____

_____

_____

_____

_____

_____

_____

_____

_____

_____

_____

_____

_____

_____

_____

_____

_____

FORGIVING ENEMIES

by Lee Strobel

YOU HAVE HEARD THAT THE LAW OF MOSES SAYS, "IF AN EYE IS INJURED, INJURE THE EYE OF THE PERSON WHO DID IT. IF A TOOTH GETS KNOCKED OUT, KNOCK OUT THE TOOTH OF THE PERSON WHO DID IT." BUT I SAY, DON'T RESIST AN EVIL PERSON! IF YOU ARE SLAPPED ON THE RIGHT CHEEK, TURN THE OTHER, TOO. IF YOU ARE ORDERED TO COURT AND YOUR SHIRT IS TAKEN FROM YOU, GIVE YOUR COAT, TOO. IF A SOLDIER DEMANDS THAT YOU CARRY HIS GEAR FOR A MILE, CARRY IT TWO MILES. GIVE TO THOSE WHO ASK, AND DON'T TURN AWAY FROM THOSE WHO WANT TO BORROW.

YOU HAVE HEARD THAT THE LAW OF MOSES SAYS, "LOVE YOUR NEIGHBOR" AND HATE YOUR ENEMY. BUT I SAY, LOVE YOUR ENEMIES! PRAY FOR THOSE WHO PERSECUTE YOU! IN THAT WAY, YOU WILL BE ACTING AS TRUE CHILDREN OF YOUR FATHER IN HEAVEN. FOR HE GIVES HIS SUNLIGHT TO BOTH THE EVIL AND THE GOOD, AND HE SENDS RAIN ON THE

JUST AND ON THE UNJUST, TOO. IF YOU LOVE ONLY
THOSE WHO LOVE YOU, WHAT GOOD IS THAT? EVEN
CORRUPT TAX COLLECTORS DO THAT MUCH. IF YOU
ARE KIND ONLY TO YOUR FRIENDS, HOW ARE YOU
DIFFERENT FROM ANYONE ELSE? EVEN PAGANS DO
THAT. BUT YOU ARE TO BE PERFECT, EVEN AS YOUR
FATHER IN HEAVEN IS PERFECT.   MATTHEW 5:38-48

Forgiving enemies runs absolutely contrary to every
impulse of human nature. When people are hit, their
knee-jerk response is to hit back—harder. So if we're
going to try to follow Christ's outlandish command to
forgive our enemies, we clearly need some help.

Associated Press reporter Terry Anderson was held
hostage in Lebanon for nearly seven years. He was chained
to a wall in a filthy, spider-infested cell. He suffered
through sickness. He endured mental torture. He longed
for his family. He was ground down by the dull ache of
incessant boredom. Through it all, he was given one
book—the Bible—and as he devoured it in a search for
words of hope, he came across what appeared to be outrageous words of hopeless naïveté: "Love your enemies!
Pray for those who persecute you!" (Matthew 5:44).

Can you imagine how outlandish that command must have seemed to Anderson after spending 2,455 mind-numbing days in cruel captivity? Love *whom?* Pray for *whom?* Show kindness toward those who brutalized me? Exhibit compassion toward those who callously extended none to me? Is Jesus a cosmic comedian or merely a starry-eyed idealist?

Finally Anderson was released on December 4, 1991. Journalists clustered around and peppered him with questions. They wanted to know what his ordeal had been like. They wanted to know his plans for the future. But then one reporter called out the question that stopped Anderson in his tracks: "Can you forgive your captors?" What an easy question to post in the abstract; what a profound issue to ponder honestly amid the grim reality of harsh injustice.

Anderson paused. Before the words of his response could come out of his mouth, the Lord's Prayer coursed through his mind: "Forgive us our sins, for we also forgive everyone who sins against us."

Then this victim of undeserved suffering spoke. "Yes," he replied. "As a Christian, I am required to forgive—no matter how hard it may be." Often it is hard. So hard, in fact, that Jesus' decree to love and pray for our opponents is regarded as one of the most breathtaking and gut-wrenching challenges of his entire Sermon on the Mount, a speech renowned for its outrageous claims. There is no record of any other spiritual leader ever having articulated such a clear-cut, unambiguous command for people to express compassion to those who are actively working against their best interests.

But wait. Hold on a moment. Maybe this command isn't so outlandish after all. Perhaps it's actually a prescription that benefits both those who forgive and those who are forgiven. Maybe there is a host of benefits that come with fostering an atmosphere of grace rather than an environment of maliciousness. The truth is, God's wisdom works. Choosing to forgive instead of to hate can turn out to be one of our greatest blessings in disguise—if we understand how this extraordinary principle works.

Jesus was very precise in choosing a word for "love" that doesn't imply emotion so much as it suggests attitude and action. As difficult as it sounds, he's urging us to have a humble, servant demeanor toward people who are our adversaries. To look for the best in them and offer help as they need it. To have a sense of goodwill and benevolence

toward them in spite of their lack of the same toward us.
To pray for their welfare and the well-being of their families. Even though we may continue to compete with them,
we are to do so fairly and respectfully, not maliciously, as
if we were trying to destroy them.

Technically we aren't being asked to like the other
person, because that would require an emotion that we
sometimes can't conjure up, despite our best intentions.
But we are, in effect, to *treat* them as though we liked
them—because that's a decision of our will. We don't
have to approve of what they are, what they've done, or
how they conduct their affairs, but we are to love *who* they
are—people who matter to God, just like you and me.
People who have failed but who are eligible for God's
forgiving grace.

In fact, the Bible says, "God showed his great love for
us by sending Christ to die for us while we were still
sinners" (Romans 5:8). Amazingly, God's response to our
rebellion against him wasn't to declare war on us as his
enemies. Instead, he returned love for evil so that the path
could be paved for us to get back on good terms with him.
And that's the kind of love he wants us to extend to those
who have sinned against us.

Eternal God,
No sword is drawn in your perfect kingdom but the
sword of righteousness, no strength known but the
strength of love. So mightily spread abroad your
Spirit that all people may be gathered under the banner of the
Prince of Peace as children of one Father. Amen.

My Thoughts and Prayers

EVERYTHING BEAUTIFUL
IN ITS TIME

by Ken Gire

GOD HAS MADE EVERYTHING BEAUTIFUL FOR ITS OWN
TIME. ECCLESIASTES 3:11

*Thou who wouldst see the lovely and the wild mingled
in harmony on Nature's face, ascend our rocky mountains.* WILLIAM CULLEN BRYANT

When we draw close to nature, reaching out to it for
clues to our existence, nature takes our hands and fills
them with the fertile loam of our humanity, reminding us
that from the earth we were taken and to the earth we will
return.

It's humbling to realize for us who have been given
dominion over nature how limited that dominion is.
We can light candles, but we can't hold back the night. We
can prepare for storms, but we can't prevent them. We

can't stop the rains in times of flood or start them in times of drought. We can't shorten winter or lengthen spring.

In Nature we are confronted with the limits of our dominion. Nowhere are those limits so obvious as in the way mountains are formed. When sheer formations of rock are suddenly thrust through the surface of the earth, we are helpless to stop it. Helpless to control either its duration or its devastation.

We are just as helpless when some tragedy devastates us. Like the death of a child. Or the diagnosis of cancer. The prodigal who runs away from home. Or the partner who walks away from a marriage. The sudden disability from a wreck. Or the sobering dismissal from work.

Upheavals come suddenly, unexpectedly, and often catastrophically. Whenever they come, however they come, they forever alter the settled terrain that once was our life. Embedded within us are physical, spiritual, and psychological layers that make up our interior landscape. When upheavals come, they alter every layer with varying degrees of destruction that sometimes take a lifetime to unearth.

Imagine for a minute that you are the landscape. The upheaval thrusts itself mercilessly through the very center of who you are. The abrading of granite. The crumbling of limestone. The crashing of boulders as they tumble down around you, shattering to pieces. You feel all of that, every grinding moment of it. Your stomach drops, your head spins, and you watch in helpless horror as the inner-most parts of your life lie on the surface, exposed to the elements.

The deafening noise is the sound of the upheaval as it forces its way through every stratified layer that lies within you. Your body, mind, emotions—all these layers are displaced. They are folded or pushed upward or thrust over each other. The social layers of your life are also shaken. And the spiritual layers that once seemed such bedrock certainties—they're shaken too. Who of us can survive the shock and aftershocks of such earthshaking experiences? Who of us has the strength to sift through the emotional rubble of the resulting devastation? Who of us has the courage to face the future, where other upheavals may await us?

Meanwhile, where is God in all of this? Didn't he see the upheaval coming? Couldn't he have prevented it—or at least warned us of it?

Much the way pressure within the earth thrusts rock

formations through its crust to create mountains, the seismic pressure of these unanswered questions creates sudden and sometimes terrifying upheavals in our faith.

To this bare and broken rock, God comes.

There the weathering grace of God begins its work, wearing granite into soil, planting windblown seeds into barren slopes, bringing life out of lifelessness and beauty out of ugliness.

Season after season the work continues.

In time God turns the most terrifying of eruptions into the most majestic of mountains, the most tragic of earthquakes into the most idyllic of landscapes.

That is the unrelenting work of heaven, to make everything beautiful in its time.

Dear Lord,

I believe you are a sovereign God, Creator of the heavens and the earth. I believe you are ruler of the universe and Lord of the landscape of my life. Every parcel of ground, no matter how small, still is within your universe and under your watchful eye. I believe that you know what happens there and that you care what happens there, especially in times of upheaval. I believe that you are good and that you work all things for good to those who love you and are called according to your purpose. *I believe that you are all-powerful and that you make everything beautiful in its time. All these things I believe, Lord. Help my unbelief.*

My Thoughts and Prayers

_____

_____

_____

_____

_____

_____

_____

_____

_____

_____

_____

_____

_____

_____

_____

_____

_____

_____

_____

_____

Why Us?

by James Dobson

O LORD, YOU HAVE SEARCHED ME
    AND YOU KNOW ME.
YOU KNOW WHEN I SIT AND WHEN I RISE;
    YOU PERCEIVE MY THOUGHTS FROM AFAR.
YOU DISCERN MY GOING OUT AND MY LYING
        DOWN;
    YOU ARE FAMILIAR WITH ALL MY WAYS.
BEFORE A WORD IS ON MY TONGUE
    YOU KNOW IT COMPLETELY, O LORD.

YOU HEM ME IN—BEHIND AND BEFORE;
    YOU HAVE LAID YOUR HAND UPON ME.
SUCH KNOWLEDGE IS TOO WONDERFUL FOR ME,
    TOO LOFTY FOR ME TO ATTAIN.

WHERE CAN I GO FROM YOUR SPIRIT?
    WHERE CAN I FLEE FROM YOUR PRESENCE?
IF I GO UP TO THE HEAVENS, YOU ARE THERE;
    IF I MAKE MY BED IN THE DEPTHS, YOU ARE
        THERE.

IF I RISE ON THE WINGS OF THE DAWN,

    IF I SETTLE ON THE FAR SIDE OF THE SEA,

EVEN THERE YOUR HAND WILL GUIDE ME,

    YOUR RIGHT HAND WILL HOLD ME FAST.

PSALM 139:1-10, NIV

*O*ne of the most breathtaking concepts in all of Scripture is the revelation that God knows each of us personally and that we are in his mind both day and night. There is simply no way to comprehend the full implications of this love by the King of kings and Lord of lords. He is all-powerful and all-knowing, majestic and holy, from everlasting to everlasting. Why would he care about us—about our needs, our welfare, our fears? Of all the situations in which we think God doesn't make sense, his concern for us mere mortals is the most inexplicable of all.

Job also had difficulty understanding why the Creator would be interested in human beings. He asked, "What is man that you make so much of him, that you give him so much attention, that you examine him every morning?" (Job 7:17-18, NIV). David contemplated the same question when he wrote, "What is man that you are mindful of him, the son of man that you care for him?" (Psalm 8:4, NIV).

Not only is the Lord "mindful" of each one of us, but he describes himself throughout Scripture as our Father. In Luke 11:13 we read, "If you then, though you are evil, know how to give good gifts to your children, how much more will your Father in heaven give the Holy Spirit to those who ask him!" (NIV). Psalm 103:13 says, "As a father has compassion on his children, so the Lord has compassion on those who fear him" (NIV). But on the other hand, he is likened to a mother in Isaiah 66:13: "As a mother comforts her child, so will I comfort you" (NIV).

Being a parent of two children, both now grown, I can identify with these parental analogies. They help me begin to comprehend how God feels about us. My wife, Shirley, and I would give our lives for our children in a heartbeat if necessary. We pray for them every day, and they are never very far from our thoughts. And how vulnerable we are to their pain! Can it be that God actually loves his human family infinitely more than we, "being evil," can express to our own flesh and blood? That's what his Word teaches.

Dear Lord,
I am overwhelmed by the thought of the great
love you have for me. In the words of the hymn,
I pray:

Great is thy faithfulness, O God my Father,
There is no shadow of turning with thee;
Thou changest not, thy compassions they fail not;
As thou hast been thou forever wilt be....
All I have needed thy hand hath provided—
Great is thy faithfulness, Lord, unto me!

My Thoughts and Prayers

BRINGING GOOD
OUT OF TROUBLE

by Josh McDowell

WE ARE PRESSED ON EVERY SIDE BY TROUBLES, BUT
WE ARE NOT CRUSHED AND BROKEN. WE ARE
PERPLEXED, BUT WE DON'T GIVE UP AND QUIT. WE
ARE HUNTED DOWN, BUT GOD NEVER ABANDONS US.
. . . SO WE DON'T LOOK AT THE TROUBLES WE CAN SEE
RIGHT NOW; RATHER, WE LOOK FORWARD TO WHAT
WE HAVE NOT YET SEEN. FOR THE TROUBLES WE SEE
WILL SOON BE OVER, BUT THE JOYS TO COME WILL
LAST FOREVER.   2 CORINTHIANS 4:8-9, 16-17

What an amazing approach to life's problems is presented
in this Scripture passage! Paul didn't run from difficulties
or try to deny they existed in order to avoid the pain. He
acknowledged his suffering, knowing that the God of all
comfort was there to ease his pain, and he viewed the
trials of life from an eternal perspective. He trusted in a

sovereign God, who would cause everything to work together for good. Paul's faith in a God who had everything under control enabled him to see the difficulties of this life as producing "an immeasurably great glory that will last forever."

At times we can even see the good that comes out of adversity in life. You can probably point to God's ability to bring honor out of hardship in your own life. He has certainly demonstrated that in mine.

After I finished seminary, I joined Campus Crusade for Christ, hoping to become a traveling youth speaker. At that time it seemed I knew no fear. I was bold, aggressive, even brash in my zeal to minister to people. But years passed, and a string of disappointing assignments brought me no closer to a ministry as a youth speaker than when I had first enlisted in Crusade. In addition, due in part to my brashness, I had offended some people in leadership positions. Thus, at a time when I believed I would finally get the kind of assignment I had hoped for, one that gave me the opportunity to speak to youth, I was assigned instead to Argentina.

I was more than disappointed; I was nearly devastated. This latest development represented more than a delay of my hopes and plans; it felt like a setback, perhaps even a reproof.

But God is sovereign, and he was already working to bring honor out of hardship. I arrived in Argentina in 1967, a time when South American universities were hotbeds of Communist activity. Brash and zealous as always, I jumped in with both feet and went head-to-head in open debate with the revolutionaries on those campuses. I traveled beyond Argentina to campuses in Bolivia and Chile. As a result, I was given the opportunity to taste some of the hardships Paul described in 2 Corinthians 4. During that two-year period, while attempting to establish a campus ministry in South America, my life was repeatedly threatened. I was robbed, falsely accused, and imprisoned. At times I wondered if I would ever make it home alive.

But if I'd ever doubted it, I learned the truth of God's promise: "My power works best in your weakness" (2 Corinthians 12:9). When I returned to the United States, American universities were just beginning to undergo the kind of unrest and upheaval that I had seen and studied for two years on South American campuses. My experience had equipped me to understand what the revolutionaries were offering as a cultural solution to American youth, and it prepared me to effectively counter that with a spiritual solution.

Had I relied on a human perspective, I could have seen my South American experience as nothing more than an unfair "exile." But my trust in God's sovereign control enabled me to submit to leadership and watch as God used two years for what they truly were: a "boot camp" to bring God honor for the next twenty years of ministry. I can say with Paul that "we know that God causes everything to work together for the good of those who love God and are called according to his purpose for them" (Romans 8:28).

Dear Lord,

When we are "pressed on every side by troubles," help us to recognize your presence. Remind us that you are a sovereign God who sees the whole picture, while we see just our present situation. Thank you for your reassuring promise of joys to come that will last forever. Amen.

My Thoughts and Prayers

_____

_____

_____

Josh McDowell

_____

_____

_____

_____

_____

_____

_____

_____

_____

_____

_____

THE MIRROR OF EVIL

by Ravi Zacharias

LET US RUN WITH ENDURANCE THE RACE THAT GOD
HAS SET BEFORE US. WE DO THIS BY KEEPING OUR
EYES ON JESUS, ON WHOM OUR FAITH DEPENDS FROM
START TO FINISH. HE WAS WILLING TO DIE A SHAME-
FUL DEATH ON THE CROSS BECAUSE OF THE JOY HE
KNEW WOULD BE HIS AFTERWARD.   HEBREWS 12:1-2

*So, in an odd sort of way, the mirror of evil can also
lead us to God. A loathing focus on the evils of our
world and ourselves prepares us to be the more startled
by the taste of true goodness when we find it and the
more determined to follow where it leads. And where
it leads is to the truest goodness of all—the goodness
of God.*   ELENORE STUMP

I found Elenore Stump's statement to be surprisingly true in
my own life. Not long ago I happened to be in Calcutta. It is a
city that shows its wounds in public. Some estimates claim
that up to two million people live on the streets—the old, the

young, even infants—hurting. The pain is so evident and so pervasive that its effect is to anesthetize one against it. Then, with some friends, I visited an orphanage operated by the order founded by Mother Teresa. As we walked in, children rose to their feet in their tiny little beds, and shouts of "Uncle!" came from different parts of the room, as little arms were raised. Our hearts melted, and tears flooded our eyes. Goodness in the face of evil is magnificent, because it is more than goodness; it is the touch of God.

Nobel Laureate Elie Wiesel relates in one of his essays an experience he had when he was a prisoner in Auschwitz. A Jewish prisoner was being executed while the rest of the camp were forced to watch. As the prisoner hung on the gallows, kicking and struggling in the throes of death, refusing to die, an onlooker was heard to mutter under his breath with increasing desperation, "Where is God? Where is he?"

From out of nowhere, Wiesel says, a voice within him spoke to his own heart, saying, "Right there on the gallows; where else?"

Theologian Jürgen Moltmann, commenting on Wiesel's story, astutely observed that any other answer would have been blasphemous.

Is there a more concrete illustration than the death of

Christ to substantiate God's presence right in the midst of pain? He bore the brunt of the pain inflicted by the wickedness of his persecutors—and showed us the heart of God. He displayed in his own suffering what the work of God is all about in changing our hearts from evil to holiness.

In fact, one of the most forgotten realities emerges from the Scriptures. Jesus struggled with the burden of having to be separated from his Father in that momentary event of his crucifixion, as he bore the brunt of evil. He cried out, "My God, my God, why have you forsaken me?" (Matthew 27:46). The incredible truth was that at the very moment his Father seemed farthest from him, he was in the center of his Father's will. That is precisely what an understanding of the Cross means. Only when one comes to the Cross and sees both in it and beyond it can evil be put in perspective.

What emerges from all of these thoughts is that God conquers not in spite of the dark mystery of evil but through it.

Mahatma Gandhi made the comment that of all the truths of the Christian faith, the one that stood supreme to him was the cross of Jesus. He granted that it was without parallel. It was the innocent dying for the guilty, the pure exchanged for the impure. Evil cannot be understood through the eyes of the ones who crucified him but only through the eyes of the crucified One. It is the woman who has been raped who understands what rape is, not the rapist. It is the one who has been slandered who understands what slander is, not the slanderer. It is only the One who died for our sins who can explain to us what evil is, not the skeptics. The Cross points the way to a full explanation.

Dear Lord,
We don't have to look far to encounter evil. Show us
your goodness in the face of evil, we pray. Let us feel
your presence in our pain. Remind us that in Christ's
death on the cross, the victory has already been won. Amen.

My Thoughts and Prayers

_____

_____

_____

_____

_____

_____

_____

AN UNNATURAL ACT
by Philip Yancey

STOP JUDGING OTHERS, AND YOU WILL NOT BE
JUDGED. STOP CRITICIZING OTHERS, OR IT WILL ALL
COME BACK ON YOU. IF YOU FORGIVE OTHERS, YOU
WILL BE FORGIVEN. IF YOU GIVE, YOU WILL RECEIVE.
YOUR GIFT WILL RETURN TO YOU IN FULL MEASURE,
PRESSED DOWN, SHAKEN TOGETHER TO MAKE ROOM
FOR MORE, AND RUNNING OVER. WHATEVER MEASURE
YOU USE IN GIVING—LARGE OR SMALL—IT WILL BE
USED TO MEASURE WHAT IS GIVEN BACK TO YOU.

LUKE 6:37-38

One weekend I sat with ten Jews, ten Christians, and ten
Muslims in a kind of encounter group led by author and
psychiatrist M. Scott Peck, who hoped the weekend might
lead to some sort of community, or at least the beginnings
of reconciliation on a small scale. It did not. Fistfights
almost broke out among these educated, sophisticated

people. The Jews talked about all the horrible things done to them by Christians. The Muslims talked about all the horrible things done to them by Jews. We Christians tried to talk about our own problems, but they paled in contrast to stories of the Holocaust and the plight of Palestinian refugees, and so mainly we sat on the sidelines and listened to the other two groups recount the injustices of history.

At one point an articulate Jewish woman, who had been active in prior attempts at reconciliation with Arabs, turned to the Christians and said, "I believe we Jews have a lot to learn from Christians about forgiveness. I see no other way around some of the logjams. And yet it seems so unfair to forgive injustice. I am caught between forgiveness and justice."

At the center of Jesus' parables of grace stands a God who takes the initiative toward us: a lovesick father who runs to meet the prodigal, a landlord who cancels a debt too large for any servant to reimburse, an employer who pays eleventh-hour workers the same as the first-hour crew, a banquet giver who goes out to the highways and byways in search of undeserving guests.

God shattered the inexorable law of sin and retribution by invading earth, absorbing the worst we had to offer—crucifixion—and then fashioning from that cruel deed the remedy for the human condition. Calvary broke up the logjam between justice and forgiveness. By accepting onto his innocent self all the severe demands of justice, Jesus broke forever the chain of ungrace.

One day I discovered this admonition from the apostle Paul tucked in among many other admonitions in Romans 12. Hate evil; be joyful; live in harmony; do not be conceited—the list goes on and on. Then appears this verse: "Do not take revenge, my friends, but leave room for God's wrath, for it is written: 'It is mine to avenge; I will repay,' says the Lord." (Romans 12:19, NIV).

At last I understood: in the final analysis, forgiveness is an act of faith. By forgiving another, I am trusting that God is a better justice-maker than I am. By forgiving, I release my own right to get even and leave all issues of fairness for God to work out. I leave in God's hands the scales that must balance justice and mercy.

When Joseph finally came to the place of forgiving his brothers, the hurt did not disappear, but the burden of being their judge fell away. Although wrong does not disappear when I forgive, it loses its grip on me and is taken over by God, who knows what to do. Such a decision involves risk, of course—the risk that God may not deal with the person as I would want. (The prophet Jonah, for instance, resented God for being more merciful than the Ninevites deserved.)

I never find forgiveness easy, and rarely do I find it completely satisfying. Nagging injustices remain, and the wounds still cause pain. I have to approach God again and again, yielding to him the residue of what I thought I had committed to him long ago. I do so because the Gospels make clear the connection: God forgives my debts as I forgive my debtors. The reverse is also true: only living in the stream of God's grace will I find the strength to respond with grace toward others.

A cease-fire between human beings depends upon a cease-fire with God.

The Lord's Prayer (Matthew 6:9-13, NKJV)
Our Father in heaven,
Hallowed be Your name.
Your kingdom come.
Your will be done
On earth as it is in heaven.
Give us this day our daily bread.

And forgive us our debts,
As we forgive our debtors.
And do not lead us into temptation,
But deliver us from the evil one.
For Yours is the kingdom and the power and the glory forever.
Amen.

My Thoughts and Prayers

_____

_____

_____

_____

_____

_____

_____

_____

_____

_____

_____

_____

_____

_____

HEARING THE
VOICE OF GOD

by Francine Rivers

HAVE MERCY ON ME, O GOD, HAVE MERCY!
I LOOK TO YOU FOR PROTECTION.
I WILL HIDE BENEATH THE SHADOW OF YOUR WINGS
UNTIL THIS VIOLENT STORM IS PAST.   PSALM 57:1

On September 11, 2001, the face of America changed
forever. Disbelief, shock, sorrow, fear, anger sent me
running again to the Word for answers to questions I couldn't
even voice coherently. *O Abba, Father, my people are dying! My
nation is under attack!* And through his Word came his voice,
soft and strong, through Old and New Testaments.

God tells us, "When you turn to me with all your
heart and with all your soul and pray to me, I hear you and
forgive your transgressions against me. I have watched for
you, beloved, and I run to meet you now. I love you! I

sent my only begotten Son, Jesus Christ, to die for you.
By grace you are saved through faith in Jesus, and I have
given you the free gift of eternal life through faith in my
Son. So don't be afraid of evil men. They can kill your
body, but they can never touch your soul. I hold you in
the palm of my hand. No one can take you away from me.

"Rest assured: my eyes are on the wicked, too. They are
not hidden from my face, nor is their iniquity concealed
from me. Pray for them to turn from their evil ways, but
know that if they do not, they are like chaff that will not stand
in the judgment. They will perish. But as for you: *serve me*.

"Do justice, love kindness, and walk humbly with me.
Remember that my eyes move to and fro throughout the
earth so that I may strongly support those whose hearts are
completely mine. Abide in me, beloved, and you will
experience the peace that surpasses all understanding. And
remember: nothing will ever separate you from me.
Neither death nor life, nor angels nor principalities, not
things present or things to come, neither powers, nor
height, nor depth, nor any other created thing can separate
you from my love. *You are mine forever.*"

In the battles ahead we must stand by faith. For if we
don't stand by faith, we won't stand at all.

Dear Lord,
We cry out to you with the words of David from
Psalm 57:

Have mercy on me, O God, have mercy!
I look to you for protection.
I will hide beneath the shadow of your wings
until this violent storm is past.

I cry out to God Most High,
to God who will fulfill his purpose for me.
He will send help from heaven to save me,
rescuing me from those who are out to get me.
My God will send forth his unfailing love and faithfulness.

I am surrounded by fierce lions
who greedily devour human prey—
whose teeth pierce like spears and arrows,
and whose tongues cut like swords.
Be exalted, O God, above the highest heavens!
May your glory shine over all the earth.

My enemies have set a trap for me.
I am weary from distress.
They have dug a deep pit in my path,
but they themselves have fallen into it.

My heart is confident in you, O God;
no wonder I can sing your praises!
Wake up, my soul!
Wake up, O harp and lyre!
I will waken the dawn with my song.
I will thank you, Lord, in front of all the people.
I will sing your praises among the nations.
For your unfailing love is as high as the heavens.
Your faithfulness reaches to the clouds.

Be exalted, O God, above the highest heavens.
May your glory shine over all the earth.

My Thoughts and Prayers

_____

_____

_____

_____

_____

_____

_____

_____

_____

_____

_____

UNDERSTANDING SUFFERING

by *Anne Graham Lotz*

O LORD, YOU ARE OUR FATHER. WE ARE THE CLAY,
YOU ARE THE POTTER; WE ARE ALL THE WORK OF
YOUR HAND.   ISAIAH 64:8, NIV

The problem of pain and questions about suffering are as
old as the human race. But they remain the clinical subject
of philosophical theories and intellectual sparring and
theological debate until they become personal—until it's
our homes or our children or our loved ones who are
hurting. Then we simply have desperate questions that
need direct answers.

What causes suffering? Is suffering due to God's
punishment for sin? The Bible clearly teaches that God's
punishment for sin is not suffering but death. Sin is so seri-
ous in God's sight that even one sin calls for the death of

the sinner. There is nothing we can do to rid ourselves of the guilt of sin in God's sight. There is nothing we can do to obtain forgiveness of sin, eternal life, or a right standing with God. Therefore we are all under God's judgment and destined for his eternal punishment because we are all sinners.

But *Jesus* stepped in and took God's punishment for your sins and mine at the cross! Because of his death for our sins, we have only to repent of our sins and accept his gift of forgiveness. Then we are absolved of guilt, our sins are atoned for, and we are saved, spared from God's wrath and punishment. He has forgiven our sins! All of our sins—*all of our sins*—have been erased from his memory! You and I need never be punished for the guilt of our sins because Jesus has already taken our punishment for us!

Therefore we do not suffer because of God's punishment for some sin we have committed.

Yet clearly some suffering *is* a result of sin. Perhaps someone has developed an ulcer because of the sin of worry and lack of trust in the Lord. Migraine headaches and psychological stress can be caused by the sin of bitterness, anger, or the refusal to forgive someone who has wronged us. We can suffer injury in a car accident as the result of disobeying the authority of the traffic laws. We might suffer through the pain of divorce if we refuse to live by God's marriage principles.

When we suffer, it's a legitimate response to examine ourselves before God to determine if we are indeed suffering because of personal sin.

It is also possible to suffer because of something one's parents have done. Every day babies are born with birth defects or drug addictions resulting from a parent's sinful abuse of sex or drugs or alcohol. Or, through a parent's physical, emotional, or sexual abuse, a child can be scarred for life.

But suffering the consequences of sin is very different from being *punished* for sin. Although we may suffer the consequences of our sins or of sins committed by our parents or someone else, suffering is not God's *punishment* for anything we might have done. Why? Because he has already punished his own Son, Jesus, for our sins.

It is possible for suffering to be the consequence of sin. But it is also possible for suffering to be *no one's fault.* Once, when Jesus' disciples were sure that a poor blind man's handicap was someone's fault, Jesus told them, "Neither this man nor his parents sinned . . . but this happened so that the work of God might be displayed in his life" (John 9:3, NIV). Sometimes the cause of our suffering may be evident; other times we may never find out the reason for our suffering. But we can know one thing for sure: Jesus cares about our suffering.

When was the last time you wept into your pillow at night, thinking no one cared? Is the pain so deep and your hurt so great that you cry night after night? Did you know that *Jesus weeps with you?* Did you know he puts all your tears in a bottle because they are precious to him? He has said that in all of your afflictions, he himself is afflicted. Why? Because *Jesus loves you!*

A good friend of mine enjoys making pottery. The process of transforming wet, pliable, dull gray clay into beautiful bowls and vases and mugs and plates is fascinating. He begins with a shapeless blob, which he places on his potter's wheel. As he spins the wheel, he gently caresses the clay, applying pressure with his fingers and palms. Beneath his skillful touch, the turning clay responds to the varying degrees of pressure until it begins to take the shape of what he has in mind. When the shape pleases him, my friend removes the clay from the wheel and paints it with beautiful designs. But the colors are dull and lifeless until he places the vessel into a kiln, where he bakes the clay for hours in extreme heat. When the pottery emerges, not only is it strong enough to use, but its colors are also brilliantly vivid. The heat transforms the weak clay into a useful vessel and transforms the dull, ugly colors into radiant beauty.

And so it is with our lives. Jesus makes suffering understandable. As the Potter, he uses suffering as the pressure on the wet "clay" of our lives. Under his gentle, loving touch, our lives are molded into a "shape" that pleases him. But the shape that is so skillfully wrought is not enough. He not only desires our lives to be useful, he also wants our character to be radiant. And so he places us in the furnace of affliction until our "colors" are revealed—colors that reflect the beauty of his own character.

Without the preparation of the loving, skillful touch of the Potter's hand, any usefulness or beauty the clay might have would be destroyed by the heat of the kiln. But Jesus makes suffering understandable to this blob of clay. In the midst of the pressure and the heat, I am confident that his hand is on my life, developing my faith until I display his glory, transforming me into a vessel of honor that pleases him! I don't trust any other potter with my life. So *please, just give me Jesus!*

Lord,
How wonderful it is to know that you love us, your
children, enough to mold us and shape us into
reflections of your glorious Son, Jesus! There is no
higher privilege for us than to allow suffering to transform us into
his likeness—even as he suffered for our sake. Amen.

My Thoughts and Prayers

_____

_____

_____

_____

_____

_____

_____

_____

_____

_____

_____

_____

_____

_____

_____

GOD WORKS
THE NIGHT SHIFT

by Ron Mehl

I WILL LIE DOWN AND SLEEP IN PEACE, FOR YOU
ALONE, O LORD, MAKE ME DWELL IN SAFETY.

PSALM 4:8, NIV

God works the night shift.

He's busy while you slumber. He's into the job while
you're into your dreams. He's fully engaged when you've
pulled the plug. The psalmist put it like this: "He who
watches over you will not slumber; indeed, he who
watches over Israel will neither slumber nor sleep"
(Psalm 121:3-4, NIV).

This is the God who moves outside our vision and
occupies himself with tasks beyond our comprehension.
His eyes peer into what we can't see; his hands work skillfully where we can only grope. This is the God who

reaches and thinks and plans and shapes and watches and controls and feels and acts while we're unconscious under a sheet and a comforter.

But don't get the idea that he's off attending to black holes and quasars or fussing with hydrogen molecules in some distant galaxy. God works the night shift *for you*. He's occupied all night long thinking about you. His interest in you never flags or diminishes—not even for a heartbeat. He is busy on your behalf even when you are not aware of it, even when you are doing absolutely nothing. When it comes to your life, he never stops observing, giving, directing, and planning. "'For I know the plans I have for you,' declares the LORD, 'plans to prosper you and not to harm you, plans to give you hope and a future'" (Jeremiah 29:11, NIV).

And me? Well, I know he's working. I know he's on the job. But lots of times I have no idea what he's doing. To be honest, there are seasons in life when he doesn't *seem* to be doing much of anything. I stare into the murky darkness of my frustration or grief or confusion, but I can't see a blessed thing.

Sometimes I want to say, "If God is at work in my life, I sure can't see it." But deep down, in my heart of hearts, I know this: Even if there are no Under Construction signs, no tracks from heavy machinery, no sounds of heavenly jackhammers in the background, the Master Architect and Builder is always hard at work in the lives of his children.

God is aware of your circumstances and moves among them.

God is aware of your pain and monitors every second of it.

God is aware of your emptiness and seeks to fill it in a manner beyond your dreams.

God is aware of your wounds and scars and knows how to draw forth a healing deeper than you can imagine.

Even when your situation seems out of control.

Even when you feel alone and afraid.

God works the night shift.

 Dear Lord,
What comfort it gives us to know that you are mindful of everything—everything—that concerns us. You are intimately involved with even the smallest details that affect our souls. May we trust in this, Lord, even when our world seems to crumble around us. Let us not forget that you still hold us in the palm of your hand. Amen.

My Thoughts and Prayers

_____

_____

_____

_____

_____

_____

_____

_____

_____

_____

_____

_____

_____

_____

_____

_____

_____

_____

_____

_____

_____

_____

THE ULTIMATE WEAPON —
PRAYER

by Doug Rumford

CONFESS YOUR SINS TO EACH OTHER AND PRAY FOR
EACH OTHER SO THAT YOU MAY BE HEALED. THE
EARNEST PRAYER OF A RIGHTEOUS PERSON HAS GREAT
POWER AND WONDERFUL RESULTS. ELIJAH WAS AS
HUMAN AS WE ARE, AND YET WHEN HE PRAYED
EARNESTLY THAT NO RAIN WOULD FALL, NONE FELL
FOR THE NEXT THREE AND A HALF YEARS! THEN HE
PRAYED FOR RAIN, AND DOWN IT POURED. THE
GRASS TURNED GREEN, AND THE CROPS BEGAN TO
GROW AGAIN.   JAMES 5:16-18

Prayer is at the very heart of every aspect of spiritual
warfare. It is the means by which we are continually
armed, supplied, directed, and restored in the battle. It
is our lifeline to our heavenly headquarters.

It is no coincidence that Paul concludes his exhortation

on spiritual armor with a call to pray: "Pray at all times
and on every occasion in the power of the Holy Spirit.
Stay alert and be persistent in your prayers for all Christians everywhere" (Ephesians 6:18).

Prayer is the essential link between us and God. It is
one of the most practical ways for us to keep our attention
riveted on the Lord, instead of being overwhelmed by the
enemy. In one of his sermons on the Lord's Prayer, Greg-
ory of Nyssa (330–395) writes about the role and effect of
prayer in a believer's life:

> The effect of prayer is union with God, and, if some-
> one is with God, he is separated from the enemy.
> Through prayer we guard our chastity, control our
> temper, and rid ourselves of vanity. It makes us forget
> injuries, overcomes envy, defeats injustice, and makes
> amends for sin. Through prayer we obtain physical
> well-being, a happy home, and a strong, well-ordered
> society. . . . It shields the wayfarer, protects the
> sleeper, and gives courage to those who keep
> vigil. . . . It will refresh you when you are weary and
> comfort you when you are sorrowful. Prayer is the
> delight of the joyful as well as the solace of the

afflicted. . . . Prayer is the enjoyment of things present and the substance of things to come.

This rich description of prayer is a long way from the trivial "give-me, give-me" prayers that mark most believers' lives. I used to think that prayer was coming to God to get what I wanted. Now I realize that prayer is coming to God to receive what he has for me. Prayer is an oasis in the desert of life. It is the power source of spiritual vitality. Understanding this broadens our concept of prayer and makes the idea of continual prayer more understandable.

The exhortation to "pray always" is repeated several times in Scripture (see Luke 18:1; 1 Thessalonians 5:17). What seems so difficult is actually commanded; therefore, it must be possible. Prayer is to be our first response, not a last resort. Too often, however, we rely on every other possible solution before turning to prayer. Once we have exhausted all human options, we finally turn to God. We must train ourselves to pray first, to pray earnestly, to pray continually. While some try to explain this away, as if *always* didn't actually mean always, I am convinced that Jesus and Paul meant just what they said: pray always!

Granted, our prayer intensity will vary depending on the circumstances, but we can develop a much more continual conversation with God than we ever thought possible.

How can you build prayer into your daily activities? This is far easier than it sounds. Start by praying when you get up in the morning, saying simply, "This is the day the Lord has made; I will rejoice and be glad in it" (see Psalm 118:24). Pray as you get dressed, asking the Lord to clothe you with the whole armor of God. Pray over your meals. Pray as you travel to school, work, or other activities, asking the Lord to direct your actions and conversation. Pray when you play, giving thanks to God for the refreshment of recreation. Practicing prayer in this way weaves a golden thread through every day, week, and year. In time you will become aware that you are praying when you had made no conscious decision to do so.

This kind of continual prayer is like a holy disinfectant, keeping spiritual viruses and infections at bay. They do not disappear altogether, but they are greatly reduced in an atmosphere that is bathed in believing prayer.

Doug Rumford

Dear Lord,
In times like these we need to pray like never before.
Make us mindful not only of ourselves but also of our
nation, our leaders, and our world. Fill us with a
passion for prayer. Let us see the signs of the times, Lord, and
partner with you to bring your kingdom to the ends of the earth.
For Jesus' sake, amen.

My Thoughts and Prayers

_____

_____

_____

_____

_____

_____

_____

_____

_____

_____

_____

_____

_____

_____

_____

TAKE COURAGE

by Lisa Ryan

GOD HAS NOT GIVEN US A SPIRIT OF FEAR AND TIMID-
ITY, BUT OF POWER, LOVE, AND SELF-DISCIPLINE.

2 TIMOTHY 1:7

*A*t the mall a few months ago, I saw a teenager wearing a T-shirt that read, "Courage—No Fear." It struck me that it should have read, "Courage—Fear. Lots of fear!"

Courage is not the absence of fear. In fact, there is no courage without fear. Our faith in Christ is simply greater than our fear. It is Christ who gives us our courage, and that courage is faith in action.

The Israelites had spent forty years wandering in the wilderness, destined for the Promised Land. Moses, who had brought them to the threshold of promise, had just died. Joshua, his young aide, was now responsible for leading the nation, and he knew from scouting reports that though this land was their destiny, they would have to fight for it and drive out their enemies one by one. Joshua must have really needed a pep talk because in this passage God tells him three times to be strong and courageous:

> *Be strong and courageous*, because you will lead these people to inherit the land I swore to their forefathers to give them. *Be strong and very courageous.* Be careful to obey all the law my servant Moses gave you; do not turn from it to the right or to the left, that you may be successful wherever you go. Do not let this Book of the Law depart from your mouth; meditate on it day and night, so that you may be careful to do everything written in it. Then you will be prosperous and successful. Have I not commanded you? *Be strong and courageous.* Do not be terrified; do not be discouraged, for the Lord your God will be with you wherever you go. (Joshua 1:6-9, NIV, emphasis mine)

Notice that God does not *suggest* courage. He doesn't say, "You might want to think about being courageous." He *commands* it: "Have I not commanded you? Be strong and courageous." That also means that courage is not a feeling. Courage is a choice.

God is looking for our willingness to go down any road he leads us—at any cost. He will supply the courage in the face of fear when we need it. "He will never leave you nor forsake you" (Deuteronomy 31:6, NIV). We can always take courage in that. When we cling to him for our strength, we will have the courage to walk in our destiny for such a time as this.

Dear Lord,

In perilous times we thank you that you have not left us without your voice. We thank you for your clear directive to us: Be strong and courageous.

We place our hope in your salvation, Lord. Grant us boldness to face the future. Amen.

My Thoughts and Prayers

_____

_____

_____

_____

_____

_____

_____

_____

Take Courage

_____

_____

_____

_____

_____

_____

_____

_____

_____

_____

_____

_____

OUR SOVEREIGN, MERCIFUL, FAITHFUL GOD

by Chuck Swindoll

THE LORD IS MERCIFUL AND GRACIOUS;
>HE IS SLOW TO GET ANGRY AND FULL OF
>UNFAILING LOVE.
HE WILL NOT CONSTANTLY ACCUSE US,
>NOR REMAIN ANGRY FOREVER.
HE HAS NOT PUNISHED US FOR ALL OUR SINS,
>NOR DOES HE DEAL WITH US AS WE DESERVE.

>PSALM 103:8-10

*M*ost people have heard at one time or another that God is sovereign, that God is merciful, that God is faithful. We hear that God rules, that God reigns. We hear that God's way is right and that it leads to glory. We hear a lot about God . . . but what does it all mean?

God's sovereignty is a mysterious doctrine at times, but it is one with great relevance for our lives. It isn't just

something for scholars and theologians to argue over.
When we say that God is "sovereign," we mean that he is
full of wisdom and knowledge, that he is in charge, that he
has total, clear perspective. He is able to see the end from
the begining; he entertains no fears, no ignorance, and has
no needs. He has no limitations and always knows what is
best. He never makes a mistake. He is invincible, infinite,
unchanging, and self-sufficient.

What does God's sovereignty mean for us? For me,
the sovereignty of God relieves me from anxiety. It
doesn't take away my questions, but it does take away my
anxiety. God's sovereignty does not mean that I am
released from responsibility. It does not mean that I have
no interest in today's affairs or that I cannot be bothered
about decisions. But when I rest in it, I am relieved of
worry.

Second, the sovereignty of God frees me from explanation. I don't have to have all the answers. I find ease in
saying at certain times, "You know, I don't know. I can't
unravel God's full plan in this." All too often, we think we
can unscrew the inscrutable. We believe we can fathom
the unfathomable. There's no depth we cannot plumb.
Well, let's face it. . . . that's not true. There are some

times when those who know the most must simply back off with hands raised and say, "It's beyond me."

I don't know why God closes some doors and opens others. I don't know how evil can be used for good. But I know ultimately that God's way is always right. It doesn't always make sense—in fact, it is often mysterious. It can seldom be explained. It isn't always pleasurable and fun. But I have lived long enough to realize that his way is always right.

Another of God's attributes that we often hear about is mercy. The beautiful thing about mercy is that it is demonstrated to the offender as well as to the victim. When the offender realizes his or her wrong, God brings mercy. When the victim needs help to go on, God gives mercy. The Bible tells us, "God is so rich in mercy, and he loved us so very much, that even while we were dead because of our sins, he gave us life when he raised Christ from the dead" (Ephesians 2:4-5). That's the ultimate example of mercy: relief from our sin. Mercy isn't passive pity. It isn't simply understanding. It isn't mere sorrow. It is a divine action on our behalf through which God brings about a sense of relief.

Mercy relieves the anguish of the grief of loss. The book of Ruth provides a wonderful example of this.

Ruth actually begins with the story of Elimelech and Naomi and their two sons. Almost immediately we read that Naomi's husband dies, apparently at a relatively young age, and she is left to raise her two sons as a single parent. When the boys are grown, both marry Moabite women. About ten years later, both of Naomi's sons die, and suddenly the family consists of three widows: a mother-in-law named Naomi and two daughters-in-law, Ruth and Orpah, grieving over the deaths of their loved ones.

Think of it. Naomi is probably still trying to get over the loss of her husband, and now she has to face the loss of her sons. And the daughters-in-law have lost their husbands. That's a lot of deaths in one family; the need for God's mercy is great. People need mercy when grief invades their lives.

> Naomi said to her two daughters-in-law, "Go back to your mothers' homes instead of coming with me. And may the Lord reward you for your kindness to your husbands and to me. May the Lord bless you with the security of another marriage." Then she kissed them goodbye, and they all broke down and wept. (Ruth 1:8-9)

Naomi says to them, in effect, "May the Lord give you mercy in your grieving. May he help you when the pain is so great that you don't know where to turn and when the lights go out at night and you have no one near to put their arms around you." God has a special mercy for those who are left as widows and widowers and for those who are left as grieving parents or grieving children.

God's will may be for you to be a Naomi. You may be the one to put your arms around the grieving and to bring relief. In those circumstances people need heartfelt compassion. They need your loving presence. So during times of grief God uses folks like us to extend his mercy as the grieving work through their sorrow.

Remember this: the Lord's mercies never cease; the Lord's compassions never fail; the Lord's faithfulness never diminishes.

Faithfulness—that's another thing we hear about. God's faithfulness simply means that he doesn't change. He will always remain faithful. In fact, he not only will not change in his faithfulness, he *cannot* change. He never cools off in his commitment to us. He never breaks a promise or loses enthusiasm. He stays near us when we are zealous for the truth, and he stays near us when we reject his counsel and deliberately disobey. He remains intimately involved in our lives whether we are giving him praise in prayer or grieving him by our actions. Whether we are running to him or from him, he remains faithful. His faithfulness is unconditional, unending, and unswerving. Nothing we do can diminish it, and nothing we stop doing can increase it. It remains great. It never diminishes. Mysterious though such incredible constancy may seem, it's true.

Trust God to remember you. He won't forget your name; he won't forget your circumstances; he certainly won't forget your prayers. He's not on the edge of heaven frantically trying to figure out who you are or thinking, *What am I gonna do with this person?* He's faithful to know exactly where you are. Trust him; he remembers you. His faithfulness won't let him forget.

Dear Lord,
Thank you that you are the sovereign Lord, that we can trust you no matter what happens. And thank you, Lord, that you grant your rich mercy to us in times of loss. Use us, Lord, to comfort those who are afraid or grieving. Allow us to tell them of your unending faithfulness. May we take comfort, Lord, in your rock-solid, eternal, unchanging love. Amen.

Chuck Swindoll

My Thoughts and Prayers

WHO PUSHES
YOUR SWING?

by Max Lucado

THEN JESUS GOT INTO THE BOAT AND STARTED
ACROSS THE LAKE WITH HIS DISCIPLES. SUDDENLY, A
TERRIBLE STORM CAME UP, WITH WAVES BREAKING
INTO THE BOAT. BUT JESUS WAS SLEEPING. THE DISCI-
PLES WENT TO HIM AND WOKE HIM UP, SHOUTING,
"LORD, SAVE US! WE'RE GOING TO DROWN!"

AND JESUS ANSWERED, "WHY ARE YOU AFRAID?
YOU HAVE SO LITTLE FAITH!" THEN HE STOOD UP
AND REBUKED THE WIND AND WAVES, AND
SUDDENLY ALL WAS CALM. THE DISCIPLES JUST SAT
THERE IN AWE. "WHO IS THIS?" THEY ASKED THEM-
SELVES. "EVEN THE WIND AND WAVES OBEY HIM!"

MATTHEW 8:23-27

Children love to swing. There's nothing like it. Thrusting
your feet toward the sky, leaning so far back that every-

thing looks upside down. Spinning trees, a stomach that jumps into your throat. Ahh, swinging!

I learned a lot about trust on a swing. As a child I only trusted certain people to push my swing. If I was being pushed by people I trusted (like Dad or Mom), they could do anything they wanted. They could twist me, turn me, stop me—I loved it! I loved it because I trusted the person pushing me. But let a stranger push my swing (which often happened at family reunions and Fourth of July picnics), and it was *hang on, baby!* Who knew what this newcomer would do? When a stranger pushes your swing, you tense up, ball up, and hang on.

It's no fun when your swing is in the hands of someone you don't know.

Remember when Jesus stilled the storm in Matthew 8? The storm wasn't just a gentle spring rain. This was a *storm.* Matthew calls the storm a *seismos,* which is the Greek word for *earthquake.* The waves in this earthquake were so high that the boat was hidden. The Sea of Galilee can create a vicious storm. Barclay tells us that "on the west side of the water there are hills with valleys and gulleys; when a cold wind comes from the west, these valleys and gulleys act like giant funnels. The wind becomes compressed in them and rushes down upon the lake with savage violence."

No sir, this was no spring shower. This was a storm deluxe. It was frightening enough to scare the pants (or robes) off of a dozen disciples. Even veteran fishermen like Peter knew this storm could be their last. So, with fear and water on their faces, they ran to wake up Jesus.

They ran to do what? Jesus was asleep? Waves tossing the boat like popcorn in a popper, and Jesus was asleep? Water flooding the deck and soaking the sailors, and Jesus was in dreamland? How in the world could he sleep through a storm?

Simple. He knew who was pushing the swing.

The disciples' knees were knocking because they thought their swing was being pushed by a stranger. Not so with Jesus. He could find peace in the storm.

We live in a stormy world. Wars rage in both hemispheres of our globe. World conflict is threatening all humanity. Jobs are getting scarce. Money continues to get tight. Families are coming apart at the seams.

Everywhere I look, private storms occur. Family deaths, strained marriages, broken hearts, lonely evenings. We must remember who is pushing the swing. We must put our trust in him. We can't grow fearful. He won't let us tumble out.

Who pushes your swing? In the right hands, you can find peace . . . even in the storm.

Dear Lord,

Thank you that you are our Father and that we are your children. We can think of no greater comfort, Lord, than to know that you, in your infinite goodness, are the One who's pushing our swing. Help us as your children to let go, to relax, to trust you, to believe that your sovereign will rules our lives, our nation, and our world. In Jesus' name, amen.

My Thoughts and Prayers

_____

_____

_____

_____

_____

_____

_____

_____

_____

_____

_____

_____

HEAVEN:
OUR CERTAIN HOPE

by Randy Alcorn

THERE ARE MANY ROOMS IN MY FATHER'S HOME,
AND I AM GOING TO PREPARE A PLACE FOR YOU. . . .
WHEN EVERYTHING IS READY, I WILL COME AND GET
YOU, SO THAT YOU WILL ALWAYS BE WITH ME WHERE
I AM.   JOHN 14:2-3

FOR WE KNOW THAT WHEN THIS EARTHLY TENT WE
LIVE IN IS TAKEN DOWN—WHEN WE DIE AND LEAVE
THESE BODIES—WE WILL HAVE A HOME IN HEAVEN,
AN ETERNAL BODY MADE FOR US BY GOD HIMSELF AND
NOT BY HUMAN HANDS.   2 CORINTHIANS 5:1

SET YOUR SIGHTS ON THE REALITIES OF HEAVEN, WHERE
CHRIST SITS AT GOD'S RIGHT HAND. . . . LET HEAVEN
FILL YOUR THOUGHTS.   COLOSSIANS 3:1-2

*B*ertrand Russell has been called the greatest mind of the
twentieth century. Anticipating his death he said, "There is

darkness without, and when I die there will be darkness within. There is no splendor, no vastness anywhere; only triviality for a moment, and then nothing."

Other than Jesus Christ himself, the greatest mind of the first century was the apostle Paul. Anticipating *his* death this is what *he* said: "To me, to live is Christ and to die is gain. . . . I desire to depart and be with Christ, which is better by far" (Philippians 1:21, 23, NIV).

Two famous men. One did not know God. The other did. When it came to their views of death, knowing God made all the difference. And so did contemplating what's on the other side of that doorway called death.

How do we know what heaven is like? Our only dependable authority is the Bible. Based on the glimpses it gives us, heaven will be beautiful and wonderful—a world that cannot be exhausted, yielding new treasures for our amazement and delight.

I've thought a lot about heaven. It has a prominent place in all my books, fiction and nonfiction. When I anticipate heaven I think of the first time I went snorkeling. Etched in my memory is a certain sound: a gasp of amazement going through my rubber snorkel when my eyes first took in the breathtaking underwater scene. There were countless fish of every shape, size, and color. And just when I thought I'd seen the most beautiful, along came something even more striking. In a far greater way, I imagine our first glimpse of heaven will cause us to gasp in amazement and delight. That first gasp will be followed by many more as we continually encounter new sights in that endlessly wonderful place.

How do we know heaven will be so beautiful and wonderful? Because the One who's prepared it for us is so creative and skillful.

Before our children were born, my wife, Nanci, and I prepared a place for them. We chose the room, picked out the right wallpaper, decorated and set up the crib just so, selected the perfect blankets. The quality of the place we prepared for our daughters was limited only by our skills, resources, and imaginations.

As he was about to leave this world, Jesus said to his disciples, "There are many rooms in my Father's home, and I am going to prepare a place for you. . . . When everything is ready, I will come and get you, so that you will always be with me where I am" (John 14:2-3).

We were made for a person and a place. Jesus is the person. Heaven is the place. And Jesus is the one building that place for us.

A good carpenter envisions what he wants to build. He plans and designs. Then he does his work, carefully and skillfully fashioning it to exact specifications. He takes pride in the work he's done and loves to show it off. And Jesus isn't just any carpenter—he's the Creator of the world we already know; he built everything we see. Heaven will be his greatest building project!

For Christians, heaven is our home. Paul said, "As long as we are at home in the body we are away from the Lord. . . . We . . . would prefer to be away from the body and at home with the Lord" (2 Corinthians 5:6, 8, NIV). Home is the place of acceptance, security, rest, refuge, deep personal relationships, great memories.

God's people, aliens and strangers on earth, spend their lives "looking forward to a country they can call their own" and "looking for a better place, a heavenly homeland" (Hebrews 11:14, 16). The capital of this heavenly country will be a "city with eternal foundations, a city designed and built by God" (Hebrews 11:10). This city will have all the freshness, vitality, and openness of the country with all the vibrancy, interdependence, and relationships of a city. A city without crime, litter, smog, sirens, seaminess, or slums.

Heaven will have an endless supply of fresh water and

delicious food. No famine or drought. Christ promised we would eat and drink with him—along with Abraham and the other patriarchs (Matthew 8:11). We will meet and converse with other inhabitants of heaven. Not only Abraham, Isaac, and Jacob, but Moses, David, Ruth, Esther, Mary, and Peter. I look forward to conversations with C. S. Lewis, A. W. Tozer, Jonathan Edwards, and Amy Carmichael.

We'll converse with angels. Because angels are "ministering spirits" who serve us (Hebrews 1:14, NIV), we'll get to know those who protected us during our years on earth.

We'll enjoy and share with others the treasures we laid up for ourselves in heaven while we lived on earth (Matthew 6:19-21). We'll open our dwelling places to others (Luke 16:9).

God gave people creativity in their unfallen state, which remained but was twisted when we fell. He will surely not give us less creativity in heaven but more, unmarred by sin, unlimited by mortality. We will compose, write, paint, carve, build, plant, and grow.

There will be no temple, no church buildings. Christ will be the focus of all. Worship will be unaffected, without pretense or distraction. We'll be lost in our worship, overcome by God's magnificence and the privilege of being his children.

In Revelation 5 we're told of a choir of angels numbering ten thousand times ten thousand—that's 100 million! And then we're told that the whole rest of creation joins these 100 million. The 100 million are merely a little ensemble on the stage. Can you imagine the power of the song?

Will we learn in heaven? Definitely. We're told that in the coming ages God will continuously reveal to us the "incomparable riches of his grace" (Ephesians 2:7, NIV). When we die, we'll know a lot more than we do now, but we'll keep learning about God and his creation and each other throughout eternity.

Will we remember our lives and relationships on earth? Of course. (We'll be smarter in heaven, not dumber!) Remembrance is important to God, which is why the heavenly city has memorials of people and events of earth (Revelation 21:12-14). It's also why God keeps in heaven "a scroll of remembrance," written in God's presence, "concerning those who feared the Lord and honored his name" (Malachi 3:16, NIV). The pain of the past will be gone. But memories of being together in the trenches, walking with Christ, and experiencing intimate times with family and friends will surely not be.

Will we know our loved ones in heaven? Certainly. We'll know even those we *didn't* know on earth, just as Peter, James, and John recognized Moses and Elijah when they joined Jesus (Luke 9:28-33), though they could not have known what they looked like. After entering heaven, the martyrs look down on earth and clearly remember their lives, fully aware of what's happening there (Revelation 6:9-11). Heaven isn't characterized by ignorance of events on earth but by perspective on them.

Heaven will offer much-needed rest to the weary (Revelation 14:13). What feels better than putting your head on the pillow after a hard day's work or kicking back to read a good book with a cold drink by your side?

But rest renews us, revitalizes us to be active again. Heaven will offer refreshing activity, productive and unthwarted—like Adam and Eve's work in Eden before sin brought the curse on the ground.

In heaven, we're told, "his servants will serve him" (Revelation 22:3, NIV). This means we'll be active, since to "serve" means to work, to expend effort, to do something. Service involves responsibilities, duties, effort, planning, and creativity to do work well.

We'll lead and exercise authority in heaven, making important decisions. We'll reign with Christ (2 Timothy

2:12; Revelation 3:21), not temporarily but "forever and ever" (Revelation 22:5). "Reigning" implies specific delegated responsibilities for those under our leadership (Luke 19:17-19). We'll rule over the world and even over angels (1 Corinthians 6:2-3).

When God brings heaven down to the new earth, he "will wipe every tear from their eyes" (Revelation 21:4, NIV). What an intimate picture—God's hands will touch the face of each individual child, removing every tear. The same verse says, "There will be no more death or mourning or crying or pain." As Thomas Moore put it, "Earth has no sorrow that Heaven cannot heal."

No hospitals. No cemeteries. No sin. No evil. No fear. No abuse, rape, murder, drugs, drunkenness, bombs, guns, or terrorism.

Heaven will be deeply appreciated by the disabled, who will be liberated from ravaged bodies and minds, and by the sick and elderly who will be free from their pains and restrictions. They will walk and run and see and hear, some for the first time. Hymn writer Fanny Crosby said, "Don't pity me for my blindness, for the first face I ever see will be the face of my Lord Jesus."

God is the creator and lover of diversity. People of

every tribe and nation and tongue will worship the Lamb together (Revelation 7:9-10).

Heaven will be the home of relentless joy. The greatest joy will be marrying our bridegroom, Jesus Christ. If we love Christ, we long to be with him. The next greatest joy will be reuniting with our departed loved ones. I don't like to be away from my family, but what keeps me going is the anticipation of reunion. The longer the separation, the sweeter the reunion. I haven't seen my mom for twenty years, my childhood friend Jerry for nine years, my dad for five. Some will be reunited with parents they've not seen for fifty years and with children lost long ago. For Christians, death is never the end of a relationship but only an interruption to be followed by glorious reunion.

C. S. Lewis said, "I must keep alive in myself the desire for my true country, which I shall not find till after death; I must never let it get snowed under or turned aside; I must make it the main object of life to press on to that other country and to help others to do the same."

Heaven is the Christian's certain hope, a hope that can and should sustain us through life's darkest hours. But this doesn't happen automatically. We must choose to think about heaven and center our lives around it: "Set your sights on the realities of heaven, where Christ sits at God's right hand. . . . Let heaven fill your thoughts" (Colossians 3:1-2).

May God give us the grace to live today as citizens of heaven, ambassadors to this foreign soil called earth. May we live today with the perspective that will be ours one moment after we die.

Dear Lord,
Thank you for the certain hope of heaven. Thank you for the incredible gift you give to those who accept Jesus' sacrifice of death for our sins. Please help us to remember that this world is not our home. Help us to remember that no matter what happens to us here, we're headed home, where a greater reality awaits us. Amen.

My Thoughts and Prayers

_____

_____

_____

_____

_____

_____

_____

_____

Reaching for God's Hand

by Stormie Omartian

$\mathcal{D}$ear Lord,

You know that when we experience great loss, it feels like a light has gone out inside of us and nothing can ever turn it back on again. We know that only you can fill that empty place in the canyon of sorrow that has been left in our hearts. Even when life as we knew it is forever destroyed, you are the one constant in our lives that can never be lost to us. All else is temporary and changing.

Our loss has brought us such pain that we wonder if we can survive it. We wonder if we will hurt forever, if we will ever feel normal again. Yet when we walk with you through our times of sorrow, we trust that you will soothe our pain, comfort our souls, heal our wounds, and fill the empty place in our hearts. We want to reach up and take your steadying hand, Lord. Please draw us close to you and lead us through this river of grief to the other side.

We know that you are a good God and that your love for us is endless. Help us to cast our whole burden of grief on you and let you carry it. Sustain us, and enable us to get beyond it. We realize that life must go on, and we ask you to help us take the next step we need to take today. We know that with you all things are possible and that your healing power can restore anything—even our broken hearts. Walk with us, Lord. We trust you to take our hands and lead us until we can feel your light on our faces and your joy in our hearts.

Amen.

Sources and Permissions

Max Lucado, "Do It Again, Lord," <http://www.maxlucado.com/read/do.it.again.html>. Used by permission of Max Lucado. All rights reserved.

Bill Hybels, "Winning through Losing," adapted from a message given at Willow Creek Community Church on September 15 and 16, 2001, entitled "Responding to a National Tragedy." Copyright © 2001 by Willow Creek Community Church. All rights reserved. Used by permission.

Chuck Colson, "God, Where Were You?" adapted from a BreakPoint broadcast on September 18, 2001, transcript # 010918. Copyright © 2001 by Prison Fellowship Ministries. All rights reserved. Used by permission.

James Dobson, "A Trustworthy God," taken from *When God Doesn't Make Sense* (Wheaton, IL: Tyndale, 1993), 20–26.

Ken Gire, "Stillness in Upheaval," taken from *The Weathering Grace of God* (Ann Arbor, MI: Servant Publications, 2001).

Skip Heitzig, "The Cross at 'Ground Zero.'" Copyright © 2001 by Skip Heitzig. All rights reserved. Used by permission.

Beth Moore, "The Lord Who Heals Us." Copyright © 2001 by Beth Moore. All rights reserved. Used by permission.

Jim Cymbala, "Pulling Up to the Table," taken from *Fresh Wind, Fresh Fire* (Grand Rapids: Zondervan, 1997), 84–86.

Max Lucado, "God's Silence, Our Questions," <http://www.maxlucado.com/read/trust.worry/index3.html>. Used by permission of UpWords and Max Lucado. All rights reserved.

Ravi Zacharias, "The Mirror of Evil," taken from *Jesus among Other Gods* (Waco, TX: Word, 2000), 134ff., 193.

Philip Yancey, "An Unnatural Act," taken from *What's So Amazing about Grace?* (Grand Rapids: Zondervan), 90–93.

Francine Rivers, "Hearing the Voice of God." Copyright © 2001 by Francine Rivers. All rights reserved. Used by permission.

Anne Graham Lotz, "Understanding Suffering," taken from *Just Give Me Jesus* (Waco, TX: Word, 2000), 174–225.

Ron Mehl, "God Works the Night Shift," taken from *God: He Works the Night Shift* (Sisters, OR: Multnomah).

Douglas J. Rumford, "The Ultimate Weapon—Prayer," taken from *What about Spiritual Warfare* (Wheaton, IL: Tyndale), 71–73.

Lisa Ryan, "Take Courage," taken from *For Such a Time As This* (Sisters, OR: Multnomah).

Chuck Swindoll, "Our Sovereign, Merciful, Faithful God," taken from *The Mystery of God's Will* (Waco, TX: Word, 1999), 80, 89, 91, 120, 125, 149.

Max Lucado, "Who Pushes Your Swing?" taken from *On the Anvil* (Wheaton, IL: Tyndale).

Randy Alcorn, "The Hope of Heaven," taken from a sermon by Randy Alcorn. All rights reserved. Used by permission.

Stormie Omartian, "Reaching for God's Hand in Times of Loss." Copyright © 2001 by Stormie Omartian. All rights reserved. Used by permission.

A full-color print of "No Greater Love," painted by Ron DiCianni (found on page vi of this book) can be obtained at www.art2see.com.